WHEN IT HURTS TOO MUCH TO WAIT

Understanding
God's
Timing

WHEN IT HURTS TOO MUCH TO WAIT

LARRY RICHARDS

WORD BOOKS
PUBLISHER
WACO, TEXAS

A DIVISION OF
WORD, INCORPORATED

WHEN IT HURTS TOO MUCH TO WAIT:
UNDERSTANDING GOD'S TIMING

Library of Congress cataloging-in-publication data:

Richards, Larry, 1931–
 When it hurts too much to wait.

 1. Christian life—1960– . 2. Consolation.
3. Time (Theology) I. Title.
BV4501.2R5126   1985   245'.4   85-22464
ISBN 0-8499-0489-7

Unless otherwise indicated, Scripture quotations are from *The Holy Bible: New International Version,* copyright 1978 by the New York International Bible Society, and are used by permission of Zondervan Bible Publishers. Scripture marked "Phillips" is from *The New Testament in Modern English*, copyright 1958, 1959, 1960, 1968 by J. B. Phillips.

Printed in the United States of America

5 67898 FG 987654321

For Sue, who felt this book must be written

Contents

There is a time for everything,
  and a season for every activity under heaven:
a time to be born and a time to die,
a time to plant and a time to uproot,
a time to kill and a time to heal,
a time to tear down and a time to build,
a time to weep and a time to laugh,
a time to mourn and a time to dance,
a time to scatter stones and a time to gather them,
a time to embrace and a time to refrain,
a time to search and a time to give up,
a time to keep and a time to throw away,
a time to tear and a time to mend,
a time to be silent and a time to speak,
a time to love and a time to hate,
a time for war and a time for peace.

Ecclesiastes 3:1–8

A Personal Word

According to Ecclesiastes, life has a rhythm. Our lives—and time itself—ebb and flow, moving in patterns that God has woven into his universe. Like a quiet tide, time carries us along, bearing us gently into paths that God's love has marked out for us.

But there are slack tides, too—endless moments when we are caught in stagnant eddies. We struggle then to hurry on, but time stands still for us. It is then, when we are gripped by unfulfilled hopes or trapped in situations with no way out, that we discover how much it hurts to wait.

This book is written for those times—times when it hurts too much to wait any longer, but when life continues to stand still. What do you and I need to understand at times like these? What can provide us with the hope that enables us to keep on despite discouragement? *When It Hurts Too Much to Wait* looks into Scripture to explore the encouragement and discover the insights God provides. Each chapter, an independent meditation, is an invitation to see your situation in a fresh, new way. Each provides guidelines to help you make your time of waiting a time of deepening spiritual and personal growth.

I hope you'll want to share your exploration of *When It Hurts Too Much to Wait* with Christian friends. The questions at the end of each chapter ("For Meditation or Discussion") will help you use this book in a Sunday school class or with a group of friends meeting in your home. The experiences you share, together with the insights God gives each of you as you explore his Word, can be a significant source of help.

But most of all, this book is for you personally, for those seemingly endless times when God's best for you is waiting, even though the waiting hurts. May God bless you and enrich your life, as he has mine, through those times when it hurts too much to wait, but wait we must for God's timing to be unveiled.

Larry Richards

WHEN
IT HURTS
TOO MUCH
TO WAIT

1

It Is for God's Glory

Sue's pillow was wet with tears.

Each night for months now she had dropped exhausted into bed and cried herself to sleep. It wasn't just the struggle with her three-year-old or the baby kicking within her womb. It wasn't just the loneliness of being in a strange town with few friends and no home church. It wasn't even the frightening prospect of having no work and carrying the responsibility of her soon-to-be two children. Sue's tears flowed because she was alone, and because she ached to love again and to be loved. She ached to be a wife again as well as a mother; she ached, and it hurt too much to wait.

But wait Sue did.

She waited while her daughter was born. She waited while she went back to school to get her teacher's certification. She waited through the long winters while she shoveled snow with arthritis-crippled hands. She waited while she taught summer school to earn money for the summer taxes and substitute-taught in the fall to earn the few dollars more that it cost to have her children cared for.

Often through the years of waiting, Sue's pillow was stained with tears, and often she woke up to find herself saying, "I wish I were dead. I wish I were dead."

When you and I look at Sue's experience, we wonder,

"Why?" Why are human beings catapulted into tragedy, and why must we so often wait so long for relief? We're excited when we see God act in our own lives or in someone else's. We can understand the blessings; after all, God loves us. But the tragedies—and the pain-filled times of waiting—are harder for us to reconcile with what we know of our Lord.

Jesus' closest friends must have wondered, too, one day in Palestine when tragedy struck a family Jesus loved.

They lived in Bethany, just a short walk from Jerusalem. If you headed east from Jerusalem and trudged up and over a few hills, before long you came to Bethany. It was just a village, but Mary and Martha lived there with their brother, Lazarus. Jesus often stopped in Bethany with his disciples. It was a quiet place. And although Martha had a tendency to bustle about and worry whether the food would be prepared just right, and Mary, the dreamy one, sometimes upset her sister by drifting off to listen to Jesus talk, their home was a place of retreat when the press of the crowds tired Jesus and he needed a place to relax and be at home.

There was a deep bond of affection linking this family and Jesus. Each one had a very special place in Christ's heart.

That's why the disciples were so surprised when the messenger came, panting and out of breath, with the word that Lazarus was deathly ill. Even the messenger's words revealed the special claim the family made on Jesus' affections: "Lord, the one you love is sick."

But when Jesus heard the message, he dismissed it: "This sickness will not end in death." The pain of the living seemed of no concern to Jesus then; the suffering of the sick hardly worth a thought. Instead, Jesus added the enigmatic phrase, "No, it is for God's glory so that God's Son may be glorified through it."

And the disciples were puzzled.

John, who tells the story in chapter 11 of his Gospel, comments on Jesus' words and actions: "Jesus loved Martha and her sister and Lazarus. Yet when he heard that Lazarus was sick, he stayed where he was two more days."

The disciples couldn't understand it.

You see, the disciples knew Jesus well. They had seen his compassion for hungry crowds expressed in the miracle of multiplying bread and fish. They had seen him moved by a leper's loneliness not just to heal, but to reach out and rest a hand on the flesh of the untouchable. They had watched Jesus hurry to help the child of a man who was a stranger and restore the sanity of a foreign madman. Surely Jesus, who had a loving personal relationship with Mary and Martha and Lazarus, would hurry to help when these loved ones had a need.

But Jesus stayed where he was.

He did not hurry to help.

He permitted his loved ones to suffer while he purposely, consciously, knowingly stayed far away.

And then, after two days, he called his disciples and told them it was time to return to Judea. It was then that Jesus showed how fully he understood the situation in the home of his loved ones. "Our friend Lazarus is asleep," Jesus explained, meaning not a natural, healing rest, but the sleep of death.

"Lazarus is dead," Jesus went on. "And for your sake I am glad I was not there, so that you may believe. But let us go to him."

This is something of the same mystery we face in our own times of agonized waiting. Through the cross, we understand how deep God's affection is for you and me. We are sure that Jesus loves us as individuals. He is at home in our families and in our hearts. And yet there are times when pain comes and Jesus seems to stay away. He who could transform our situation with a word or with a touch purposely, consciously, knowingly remains where he is. He lets us experience the pain while he—and time itself—seems simply to wait.

The disciples probably guessed at reasons why Jesus waited. John 11 suggests one theory they probably discussed while squatting outside the house where they were staying, across the Jordan river from Jerusalem and Bethany.

We can visualize Thomas, the doubting disciple, nodding wisely and saying what the other eleven were thinking: "He can't go back now, you know—the priests." And they all nodded with him, remembering.

Jesus had led his followers over the Jordan after another crisis in Jerusalem. The leaders of Israel had confronted Jesus in the Temple. "If you are the Christ," they had demanded, "tell us plainly."

And Jesus had done as they asked. He had reminded them that he had already told them who he was, but they had not believed. He had also reminded them of the miracles he had performed, each of which testified of Jesus' special relationship with God the Father. And then Jesus had promised those who did believe in him eternal life, sealing the promise with the announcement that "I and the Father are one."

The leaders had understood all too well. They had snatched up paving stones, intending to stone Jesus to death because his words were a clear and unequivocal claim to be God.

But Jesus had escaped, leading his followers out of the city and across the Jordan to safety. Behind him, in Jerusalem, the furious leaders had continued to fume and plot, committed now more than ever to bringing about Jesus' death.

And so the disciples nodded wisely. We can imagine their remarks: "Of course Jesus can't go to Bethany. Why, it's just two miles from Jerusalem."

"Too dangerous," we can almost hear another agree. "He'll wait till things calm down."

Then, just when the disciples were sure they had Jesus' motives all figured out, the Lord told them, "Let us go back to Judea."

The twelve objected. "But Rabbi," John reports them as saying, "a short while ago the Jews [John's term for the leaders of Israel—not the Jewish people] tried to stone you, and yet you are going back there?"

The return to Judea was filled with potential danger for Jesus and his followers. But Jesus explained the urgency: "Our friend Lazarus has fallen asleep; but I am going to wake him up."

And then Thomas showed his courage, as well as his tendency to look pessimistically and doubtfully at life. "Let us also go," Thomas said, "that we may die with him."

The disciples' theories about why Jesus had delayed were clearly wrong; it had not been fear that had kept him from going to Lazarus and Mary and Martha in their need. Aware now that their best reasoning had failed them, the disciples could only follow where Jesus was about to lead.

This incident touches something important in our approach to life. Each of us struggles to make sense of our experiences. We probe to find reasons for what happens to us. When God seems far away or inactive, we feel we need to understand why.

Like the disciples, we may invent reasons. Our explanations of God's motives and choices may even be plausible. But the true reason for God's silence while we are going through tragedy or waiting in agony for a glimmer of light will always be a mystery. We may be confident that God has a purpose, and that his purpose for us will ultimately prove to be good. But what that purpose is we simply cannot know.

For Sue, deserted after eight years of marriage, pregnant,

and with a three-year-old boy, no good reason for God's silence suggested itself. She found a church and went there Sundays, eyes often filling with tears as she saw the congregation's solid couples seated side by side all around her. Even meeting with the family of God reinforced the awareness that she was alone, and tears slipped down her cheeks again and again on Sunday mornings. There were no reasons she could imagine for what had happened to her, and so she could only walk step by step, trusting that Jesus was with her on the journey and leading her along a path that he alone knew.

Perhaps it's easier, when times of waiting come, not to build theories or try to understand. Perhaps it's best simply to wait, assured that when the time is right, Jesus will speak. "Let us go," he'll say. And then the waiting will be replaced by movement as life moves on in the direction God has had in mind all along.

"I am going to wake Lazarus up," Jesus says. The time of waiting will be over, and we'll awaken to Jesus' fresh, new day.

When Jesus arrived in Bethany, Lazarus had been in his tomb for four days. Martha, hearing that Jesus was approaching, ran to meet him. "Oh Lord," she sobbed, "if you had only been here!" "If you had been here, my brother would not have died. But I know that even now God will give you whatever you ask."

Jesus said quietly, "Your brother will rise again."

Martha, hurting and yet sustained by the hope shared by pious Jews then as well as Christians today, replied, "I know he will rise again in the resurrection at the last day."

Then, fixing Martha with a compelling gaze, Jesus spoke words that she heard but did not really understand. "I am the resurrection and the life. He who believes in me will live, even though he dies; and whoever lives and believes in me will never die. Do you believe this?"

Martha quickly affirmed her faith: "I believe that you are the Christ, the Son of God." And then Martha hurried off to get her sister.

The poignant scene was repeated with Mary. Mary fell at Jesus' feet and she, too, said, "Lord, if you had been here, my brother would not have died." And Mary's grief spilled over again in great, anguished sobs.

The Bible tells us that Jesus shared their sorrow. He was troubled, deeply moved. And, according to the shortest verse in our Bible, "Jesus wept."

It was then, as the tears streamed down Jesus' expressive face, that onlookers said, "See how he loved him!" and wondered aloud, "Could not he who opened the eyes of the blind man have kept this man from dying?"

And Jesus could have.

But Jesus did not.

Despite the anguish he felt at the suffering of his loved ones, Jesus, too, had waited. He had waited for the right moment, for God's timing, that a greater good might come.

Lazarus, according to the custom in Palestine in that day, was buried in a rock tomb that was sealed with a great carved stone. The day Lazarus had died he had been wrapped in strips of linen cloth, and spices had been bound next to the body. Bodies decompose quickly in Palestine, even in winter, so Lazarus's body had been carried immediately to the tomb and the rock seal had been rolled in place. The mourners wept outside—and would continue to weep for at least seven days—as the loved one's body began to lose human shape and the earthly element began its return to dust.

Standing outside Lazarus's tomb, Jesus wept with the mourners. And then he spoke.

"Take away the stone!"

Then Martha, whose faith was strong, cried out, "But Lord! By this time there is a bad odor, for he has been there four days."

Jesus looked at Martha and reminded her, "Did I not tell you that if you believed, you would see the glory of God?"

No one else dared to object.

They rolled back the stone.

Lifting his eyes to heaven, Jesus thanked God the Father for hearing him. And in a loud voice, Jesus called to the dead Lazarus.

"Lazarus, come out!"

In the awed silence that fell, the family and their friends could hear first the stillness, then the rustle of movement within the tomb. There was the shuffle of feet, and then Lazarus appeared at the door, still wrapped in the grave clothes.

Then, before the sounds of joy could resound from that hillside to fill the home of Mary and Martha and the restored Lazarus—to overflow from Bethany and resound even in Jerusalem—Jesus said simply, "Take off the grave clothes and let him go."

The time of waiting was over.

The glory of God filled Palestine's hills, as anguish gave birth to joy.

During the years that Sue wept into her pillow, she couldn't imagine joy.

Waiting is like this for all of us. The pain of our present fills us, and unless we make a conscious effort to remember, pain leaves no room for hope or even faith.

Often, when it hurts too much to wait, we treat our relationship with Jesus much as Martha did. Oh, Martha believed that Jesus is the Christ, the Son of God. She believed that this life will be followed by another, as resurrection forever defeats man's final enemy. But somehow Martha failed to expect Jesus to work *in her here and now.* She held his promise, "Your brother will rise again," at arm's length and relegated it to the distant future.

Martha had forgotten that resurrection is found in Jesus himself, that he *is* the resurrection and the life. When we live in relationship with Jesus, there is always hope for us in our here and now. Resurrection power flowing from our Lord can transform every human situation and turn sorrow to overflowing joy, to the glory of God.

There came a time for Lazarus when he heard Jesus' voice call to him in his tomb. And there will come a time for all of us when we will hear Jesus lovingly say that our own waiting time is over. We know the pain of waiting. But we will experience the joy that comes when waiting gives birth to the good that God has conceived for you and me.

Today, even Sue's years of anguished waiting are past, swallowed up in joy. The loneliness is gone, and she lives with her new husband, who loves her and her children.

We can be encouraged by stories such as Sue's, which show that God's timing is designed to bless us in the end. But it may be that when we are gripped by the pain of waiting, we most need to remember John's report of Jesus and Lazarus. Meditating on that story offers us a solid basis for the hope that we, too, will find joy after pain.

What can we discover in John 11 that we can hold on to when it hurts too much to wait any longer?

(1) *The bond that we establish with Jesus is deep and unbreakable.* Lazarus and Mary and Martha were more than friends to Jesus. Again and again John 11 reminds us that Jesus *loved* them.

Faith brings you and me into this same love relationship with our Lord. Paul catches the wonder of it in Romans 5. "You see," he writes, "at just the right time, when we were still powerless, Christ died for the ungodly. Very rarely will anyone die for a righteous man, though for a good man someone might possibly dare to die. But God demonstrates his own love for us in this: while we were still sinners, Christ died for us" (vv. 6-8).

When the pain of waiting makes us doubt the reality of God's love, we can remember the timing of Jesus' death. It was when we were powerless, caught in the web of sin. Even then, knowing us as we were, Jesus died for us.

Bonded to Jesus now by our response to his great act of sacrificial love, we can be assured of his commitment to us.

The anchor of our relationship with God is not our love for him or any of our subjective feelings, but the reality of his love for us. As John says, "This is love: not that we loved God, but that he loved us and sent his Son as an atoning sacrifice" (1 John 4:10).

(2) *Divine delays do not indicate abandonment.* It must have felt that way to Mary and Martha and looked that way to the disciples, who theorized that Jesus was putting his personal safety ahead of the needs of his friend Lazarus. But Jesus had his own purpose in waiting. Not only was the raising of Lazarus from death a greater evidence of God's glorious power; it also created a greater joy and wonder in the hearts of Jesus' loved ones.

There are times when we can only appreciate the Lord, and only appreciate the good things he gives us, when our blessings stand in contrast with our suffering.

God's timing, even when the waiting is long and painful, never means abandonment, but always promises a greater joy to follow.

(3) *We never suffer or wait alone.* This would have been hard for Sue to grasp during the years after her abandon-

ment. But the emotions of Jesus, unveiled by John, reassure us. Jesus was "deeply moved" by the pain experienced by the friends of Mary and Martha and Lazarus. He was "troubled," and he "wept."

Every observer of that scene understood the emotions Jesus displayed. He was sharing the hurt and pain of those who were suffering, because love compelled him to enter into their experience.

When you and I hurt, Jesus is near, even though he may seem far away. He is with us, entering into our experience, feeling the hurt with us and sharing the suffering.

God's love guarantees his presence with us and his empathy in every difficulty.

You and I may never understand just why a particular waiting time was part of God's plan for us. We may never understand his grand purpose in our pain. But when we must wait, we can be assured that:

- the bond of love we establish with Jesus is deep and unbreakable.
- divine delay does not indicate abandonment.
- we never suffer or wait alone. Jesus is with us, sharing in our every experience, waiting only on God's timing to transform our pain into joy.

For Meditation or Discussion

1. Recall the time of waiting that has been most difficult for you. In what ways did that time and your experience parallel the experience reported in John 11?

2. What is hardest for you about waiting? What do you see in the story of Jesus and Lazarus that is most helpful to you personally?

3. Can you find one verse in John 11 that you believe would be helpful to others who are trapped in a time of pain-filled waiting? What is there about that verse that would minister to such a person?

2

The Set Time

Twenty-nine is too late.

That's what Pam thought. Pam, who only wanted to be a wife and mother. Pam, locked for nine years in a job as a police dispatcher. Pam, who fell in love with a fellow officer, only to discover later that he was married. Pam, who struggled for years with the feelings and the natural urges that surged so powerfully, especially when she was lonely, and when her work threw her into renewed contact with "him."

There were moments when the years of empty waiting were too much for Pam. She is normally cheerful and attractive, but there were times when the passage of another month with no prospect of any change seemed like a crushing weight. Sometimes Pam saw endless tomorrows, empty nights, stretching out to touch her life's horizon. And the vision was too painful for anything but tears.

If you can feel with Pam the weight of nine long years of frustration and discouragement, with no prospect even now for the fulfillment of her dreams, you can understand her words to Sue:

"Twenty-nine is too late. If something doesn't happen by my next birthday, I'm not going to wait any longer. I'm just going out and do what I want to do."

There's a panic that grips us when, after what seems ages of waiting, the pressures within us shout that even another moment is just too much. That panic is a sign: a sign that the time of resolution is drawing near. It is also a warning: a red light set to flashing within us, God's voice urging us not to act foolishly.

The red light was flashing in King Saul, too, as he stood one late afternoon on a rocky outcrop crowning a hill at Gilgal. The sun flooded the valley and the opposite hillside with crimson, glowing fiercely on the sharpened edges of iron weapons gripped by thousands of Philistines camped there.

Saul was about Pam's age, thirty years old. Like Pam, Saul was attractive, a handsome man who stood a good head taller than the people who had recently confirmed him as their king. The bright hope of his generation, Saul faced an awesome challenge. But he faced it boldly, and with confidence in God.

For years the Israelites had been oppressed by their Philistine neighbors. Israel then lived as isolated tribes held together by their common heritage and common faith, but without national identity. Their neighbors, a seacoast people who had swept along the shores of the Mediterranean, establishing colonies that grew into powerful, unified nations, maintained their superiority by a monopoly on iron. They guarded the secret of working iron so carefully that the Israelites were forced to come down from their hills and valleys to the coastal plains just to have the metal strips that edged their wooden plows sharpened by their oppressors. In the whole force that Saul could muster for battle, only Saul himself and his son, Jonathan, had iron weapons.

And yet Saul had boldly challenged the enemies who had attacked his people. In his first test as king, when the powerful Ammonites besieged Jabesh Gilead, Saul had rallied Israel. Showing a surprising grasp of military tactics, Saul had led Israel to victory (see 1 Sam. 11). And the triumphant Saul modestly had given the credit to God, reminding his people that "this day the Lord has rescued Israel."

Saul's own history had given birth to this attitude. Although an impressive young man, Saul had had no political aspirations until God's prophet, Samuel, privately anointed him and said, "the Lord anointed you leader over his inheritance." Samuel had then told Saul, "The Spirit of the Lord will come upon you in power, and you will prophesy . . . and you will be changed into a different person."

So Saul, at thirty, undoubtedly fearful and yet strengthened by the clear evidence that God was with him, had faced his challenges with a bold courage and a decisive will to act. And Samuel's prophetic words had come to pass. Saul had been acknowledged as king, and he had passed his first military test with a victory he credited to the Lord.

The only thing that Saul could not face was . . . waiting.

In some ways you and I tend to look back in awe on Bible characters. They seem larger than life in their strengths and in their weaknesses. We idolize David, admire Moses, stand in awe of Paul. We draw lessons from their lives, and perhaps secretly envy them for their intimate relationship with God and for the glowing strength of their faith. We even find much to admire in the flawed characters of Scripture. The Jonahs and the Sauls were persons of faith, too, and have won a place on the roll of history's heroes.

There is nothing wrong with looking at the characters of the Bible this way. Their stories were given us as models and examples of how to live and how not to live. But in our preoccupation with biblical characters, it may be too easy to forget the special heroism of ordinary lives.

Pam doesn't think of herself as a heroine. She might grant Saul a place on the roster of great men, but would never see herself as great, too. And yet, compare.

Saul stood waiting on the brow of Gilgal's hills for just

a few short days. He looked across the valley, and the sight of the assembled Philistine hordes filled him with fear. As the days passed and he continued to stare at his enemy, the moment of his panic came.

But Pam stood waiting for nine years. She looked across the valley to see nothing but *more* years marching toward her, enemies all, each gripping as weapons three hundred sixty-five empty nights and three hundred sixty-five meaningless days. And during those nine long years of waiting, although she had moments of despair and times when her forced choices were unwise, she waited with courage and in faith, facing her personal enemy. The waiting, as painful as it remained, in some measure qualified Pam for the heroine's mantle, even as your waiting and mine qualifies you and me.

Waiting has the strange power of infusing the ordinary with greatness, of infusing the common with a witness to the strengthening glory of God.

Saul, waiting on the hilltop, struggled with excruciating inner pain. He had been successful so far, but what would a defeat mean? Although Israel had rallied to him in victory, he was sure they would desert him unless their trust was confirmed by yet another triumph.

And defeat seemed certain this time.

At Jabesh Gilead, the whole nation had mustered behind Saul. Some three hundred thirty thousand men, ill equipped but made powerful by their numbers, had crushed the Ammonites. Now Saul had with him only three thousand troops—with which he had attacked a Philistine outpost and provoked the Philistines into massive response.

And massive it was. The Philistines had called out three thousand chariots (the tanks of the ancient world), and "soldiers as numerous as the sand on the seashore."

Saul had responded to the Philistines' challenge by

sending messengers throughout Israel. But this time there
had been no response! The word had been whispered in
all of Israel's scattered villages that Saul had acted foolishly
and stirred up the Philistines. Terrified, the citizens who
were Saul's hope had scurried off to hide "in caves and
thickets, among the rocks, and in pits and cisterns." Some
had even left their homeland, slipping over the Jordan river
to take refuge in distance.

The modern image of a Western town deserting its sheriff
when the bad guys come is hardly new! Saul experienced
all that those movie sheriffs are supposed to feel as they
wait, futilely, for their citizen-deputies to turn out.

As Saul waited, watching the enemy forces assemble, the
Bible says that "all the troops with him were quaking with
fear." Gradually, even the small army of three thousand
that Saul had personally recruited began to scatter.

Now, there was one great difference between Saul's waiting and Pam's. Pam waited for years, never knowing when
her waiting might end. Saul was waiting for only a brief,
set time.

The prophet Samuel, Saul's confidant and friend, had
sent a message to Saul with words to this effect: "I'll be
there within seven days." When he came, this prophet who
was also a priest would offer sacrifice to God and call on
the Lord to help. And presence of the man of God might
reinstill courage in Saul's troops, even as his prayers might
move God to intervene.

But days passed, and Samuel did not come. More of Saul's
men slipped away. Nights came and went, and even the
ashes of Saul's hope that Israel might respond to his call
for help grew dead and cold.

At dawn the seventh day Saul took his post on the craggy
top of the hill. He gazed pensively down, somberly measur-
ing the ever-growing strength of the Philistine host and
glancing again and again back toward the path that Samuel

must climb to join him. Morning brightened and warmed. Noon came, but the hot sun that beat on Saul's back went unnoticed as an icy fear tightened its grip on the king. Then the sun crested and began its downward slide toward the Mediterranean.

We can see Saul's lieutenants nervously sidle up to the tense figure of the king, bringing fresh reports of new desertions.

Finally Saul could stand it no longer.

He acted.

"Bring me the burnt offering and the fellowship offerings," Saul commanded. As his men scurried to obey, Saul set aside his warrior garb and took the sacrificial knife.

Saul finished the sacrifices and stood back, watching the smoke from the altar ascending like some uninvited prayer into heaven. It was then that Samuel arrived, pushing his aging body to its limits as he, too, saw the smoke and flames.

"What have you done?!" the old prophet cried.

Surprised at his mentor's passion, Saul explained. "When I saw that the men were scattering, and that you did not come at the set time, and that the Philistines were assembling at Micmash, I thought, 'Now the Philistines will come down against me at Gilgal, and I have not sought the Lord's favor.' So I felt compelled to offer the burnt offering."

This is the key to the panic that comes when the pressure of waiting builds to an unbearable peak. Saul said it first: "I felt compelled. I just couldn't wait any longer. I had to act."

Pam said the same thing to Sue: "Twenty-nine is too late. If something doesn't happen by my next birthday, I'm not going to wait any longer. I'm just going out and do what I want to do."

But it is just when we feel most compelled to act that we must try the hardest to wait! As the pressure of waiting

becomes unbearable, those feelings of panic should serve
as God's flashing light to warn and to reassure us. For
often they are an indication that we are approaching God's
set time, that if we can wait just those moments more we
will see him act for us.

And so it was that Samuel rebuked a surprised Saul:
"You acted foolishly."

God, through Samuel the prophet, had commanded Saul
to wait seven days. And Saul *had* waited, but not the full
time. God, through Samuel the priest (authorized in Israel
to offer the blood sacrifice that testified to forgiveness and
to fellowship with the Lord), was waiting, too—to answer
prayer. But Saul had violated the Old Testament's Law and
usurped the role reserved for Israel's priesthood.

"You acted foolishly."

The word in Hebrew here is *sākal*. It means "foolish,"
but in a moral or spiritual sense rather than in an intellectual
sense. Saul looked at his circumstances and unquestionably
evaluated his situation well—the situation was desperate!
But strangely, despite his personal experiences with the
Lord, all Saul had been able to see were the reddened edges
of the enemy iron and his own dwindling forces. Saul seemed
unaware of spiritual realities and unconcious of the power
God holds available, ready to unleash at his set time.

The fifteenth verse of 1 Samuel 13, which records this
story, underlines Saul's insensitivity. The Bible tells us that
when Samuel left Gilgal, Saul counted the men who were
(left) with him. "They numbered about six hundred."

Six hundred.

We don't know if that number stirred Saul's memory,
but it speaks to our own. We remember stories that Saul
himself must have heard—stories of Gideon, who like Saul
had been called by God to lead Israel in a time of enemy
oppression.

Reassured by repeated evidence that God was with him, Gideon had gathered a large force to attack the invading Midianites. But bit by bit God had whittled away Gideon's numbers. First, Gideon had been told to send home anyone who was doubtful or afraid. Then he had been told that even the few thousand who remained were too many. "Lead your army through a river," God told Gideon. Only those who snatched up water in their cupped hands as they hurried through the stream had been permitted to remain. Their number? Three hundred.

And so with three hundred men—half the number that remained with Saul—and those three hundred armed only with trumpets and torches, God had delivered his people.

With a full six hundred, God could have worked the defeat of countless Philistines, despite the enemy's chariots and weapons of iron.

"You acted foolishly."

Saul acted foolishly because he remained insensitive to the reality of God, and to the power of God to transform any situation and bring his people victories grand beyond their dreams.

Pam didn't act foolishly.

Oh, the fears were there, as real and as intense as Saul's fears. The enemy was there, too—those years assembled across the valley, mustering countless empty days and sterile nights. But though the panic came, and Pam felt compelled to act, she continued to wait.

And then God acted.

Today Pam is excited and enthusiastic. She's been accepted at the University of Michigan's graduate school of social work, ready to work toward a degree that will qualify her to work with juveniles and in various prison settings. Door after door has miraculously opened—money, housing, contacts—and Pam clearly sees God's hand guiding her to prepare in an area of long-term interest for her—the criminal justice system.

Will Pam marry? Probably—when God brings her in contact with the right man. But until God's set time comes for marriage, Pam rejoices that the Lord has transformed her view of her future.

Looking ahead, Pam now sees meaningful tomorrows— friends instead of enemies. She sees busy times of growing and serving as she follows the path that, at long last, Jesus has set before her.

Saul's life and Pam's are set in contrast for us. This is how I believe we are supposed to approach a study of the life of Saul. The history of Israel's first king—and of the tragedies evoked by his spiritual insensitivity—is not intended to frighten us. It is not intended as some grim threat, a warning that God will crush you and me should we, too, step out of line.

No, Saul's life is intended to encourage us, to remind us that what might have been for him can be for you and me!

What are we to learn, and how are we to respond, in those moments when the pressures mount and we feel compelled to act because we can't wait any longer? Here are some things to remember:

(1) *God has a set time for you and me.* However it may seem, waiting isn't endless for God's people.

While Saul was told the specific limits of God's timing, most of us must live without this kind of information. In a way, our uncertainty is a blessing. If God's set time involves years, we are protected from that knowledge. If God's set time is tomorrow, then we will be surprised by its joy and will savor its unexpectedness.

Protected from knowing the specific dates and times when

God will act, we are invited simply to live in hope. God wants only the best for his loved ones. He has his own set time in mind when he will act for us. Until then, even though it hurts to wait, waiting is wisest and best.

(2) *Mounting pressure is often an indication that God's set time is near.* This isn't always true. Often you and I feel the pressure of waiting in repeated surges. But each of us has experienced the mounting of an almost unbearable pressure, the growth of a panic that stretches our emotions tight.

It is just this kind of experience which signals that the purpose of our wait is about to be fulfilled. If Saul had only found the strength to wait one brief hour, Samuel would have arrived and Saul himself would have been confirmed as founder of an Israelite dynasty. But in Saul's case, the pressure revealed the flaw in his character; the superficiality of his faith. God's good purpose for Saul was thwarted as Saul failed waiting's final test.

But for Pam, and for you and me, the pain and panic of waiting will have a different outcome. Because we continue to wait, despite the hurt, and refuse to act foolishly, you and I will receive the good God has in mind for us. We will be strengthened through the pain of waiting, and then we will be filled with thankful joy when we discover the release God has prepared.

(3) *Wisdom reminds us of the goodness and resources of God.* Wisdom here is the opposite of foolishness. And both have to do with our comprehension of spiritual realities.

The foolish believer stares despondently at his or her circumstances. The present situation seems to the foolish to be hopeless, and the grim realities of life block every prospect of relief.

The wise believer looks at circumstances realistically. But

to the wise, the ultimate reality is God—not the present circumstance. The God of Gideon, who can put great armies to flight with a handful of men, is not limited by our circumstances. Our God is free to act, to change our situation or to change us, giving us a new perspective and a new life path that provides our yearned-for release.

To "act foolishly" is to be pressured by our circumstances to act hastily, without God's guidance, without the sense of his hand resting again on our shoulder. To act foolishly is to be forced by our panic to take actions that deep down we feel are wrong, or to expect in the momentary pleasures of sin a satisfaction that can only be found in righteous joys.

Our times of waiting, and the pressures that mount as God's set time draws near, call for us to act with great wisdom. When the panic comes, we are to remember the power and goodness of our God and to hold back until circumstance or an inner certainty tells us that at last his time has come for us to act.

And so in our times when the pressure of waiting is intense—whether they be hours or days or even years—we can keep on waiting with confidence.

God has a set time for you and me.

The panic we feel may well be an indication that his set time is near.

And wisdom, our sensitivity to spiritual realities, reassures us by calling to mind both the goodness and the resources of our God.

For Meditation or Discussion

1. Remembering the story of Gideon might have provided Saul with the insight he needed in order to act wisely.

What Bible story or event or verse has given you insight and strength when you have been under pressure?

2. Think of yourself as a hero or heroine, like Pam. What might be written on God's citation awarding you a place among his great men and women of waiting faith?

3. What is the single most important insight you can find in the story of Saul's failure as it is told in 1 Samuel 13:1–15?

3

He Will Act

Eileen was on the phone.

Her voice, drained of all energy, carried that deadening sense of despair that Sue recognized all too well.

"Listen," Sue told her. "It's not going to be like this always. You're lonely now and feeling sorry for yourself. Nothing seems worthwhile. But things will get better."

The silence that followed carried the message of Eileen's disbelief.

"I know just what you're thinking," Sue went on. "You're thinking, 'That's all right for her to say. She's found a new husband, and she's loved.'" Eileen laughed, a little sheepishly.

"I know, because I remember how a friend of mine told me the same things I'm telling you. I didn't believe her then, either, and I thought, 'You can say that. You're married to someone who loves you.' But you know something, Eileen? She was right. And I learned to believe even when I didn't believe."

Sue had met Eileen at a "Coping with Divorce" seminar provided by a Christian ministry in the city where she lives. After Sue's husband left and her daughter was born, Sue had attended the same seminar, and the ten weekly meetings had helped her understand both her feelings and the practical problems she would have to face as a newly single person. Later, Sue had become involved with the ministry as a coordinator of monthly meetings for singles held in various sections of the city. Now, continuing to care after her own remarriage, Sue has recently given her Tuesday nights to serve as an enabler in a small group of those now taking the "coping" seminar.

Eileen is a member of Sue's small group. A woman who had been overly dependent on her husband during their long marriage, Eileen feels lost without him. When her husband left her, Eileen didn't know how to fill the gas tank of a car. She had never paid a bill. Her husband even told her what to make for meals and when to do the family laundry. While Eileen resented his domination, she also depended on it. Now, forced to cope with life on her own, she feels her helplessness and she despairs.

Eileen is a person who is waiting. A Christian, Eileen waits, not knowing how or what to believe. Talking with her on the phone that evening, Sue shared something about how to believe when we simply do not believe.

Psalm 37 is one of Scripture's richest sources of simple words on belief. Those words are appropriately cast in terms of trust.

Ultimately, this is what a biblical faith is. It is not belief that a particular thing is true or assurance that certain events happened. Of course, truth and history are vital in our faith, but the central reality of Christian faith remains trust in a Person. The central reality is our relationship with the Person who is our Truth and who acts in human history. And so Psalm 37 brings us words of encouragement, helping us learn how to trust when the pain of waiting robs us of the power to believe:

Trust in the Lord and do good (v. 3).

Commit your way to the Lord;
  trust in him, and he will do this (v. 5).

Be still before the Lord and wait patiently for him (v. 7).

Wait for the Lord and keep his way,
  he will exalt you to possess the land (v. 34).

The salvation of the righteous comes from the Lord;
  he is their stronghold in time of trouble (v. 39).

In each of these verses, and in others from this enriching psalm, "the Lord" is the focus. He is the central reality that we are to fix in our minds as we wait—patiently at times and all too impatiently at others. If we are to trust when we can't believe, we must begin by reexamining our view of just who our God is.

This was critical for God's Old Testament family at one of sacred history's turning points. Israel was a slave people in Egypt. For some four hundred years, the Jewish people had passed on tales of a God who had spoken centuries before to Abraham and Isaac and Jacob, and who had given those patriarchs great promises. But for hundreds of years, the chosen people had been merely slaves, forced to labor for the oppressors in whose land they were trapped.

Then, in God's own time, an aged shepherd was suddenly confronted by a Voice from a flaming bush. Told to return to Egypt, this shepherd, Moses, was commissioned to be Israel's deliverer.

Moses objected. But God continued to insist. "I have indeed seen the misery of my people in Egypt. I have heard them crying out because of their slave drivers, and I am concerned about their suffering. So I have come down to rescue them . . . and to bring them up out of that land into a good and spacious land, a land flowing with milk and honey" (Exod. 3:7–8).

Moses still hesitated.

"Suppose I go to the Israelites and say to them, 'The God of your fathers sent me to you,' and they ask me, 'What is his name?' Then what shall I tell them?"

God's answer established forever the way that you and I are to view our Lord.

"I am who I am. This is what you are to say to the Israelites: 'I AM has sent me to you'" (vv. 13–14).

What is so significant about this response? Simply that it is the basis for the Old Testament's personal name for God: Jahweh. The Old Testament has many different terms *describing* God: "the Almighty," "Sovereign Lord," "God of Abraham," and so on. But Jahweh is God's personal name, just as Larry is my personal name and "author" or "Ph.D." are simply descriptions. In giving us his personal name, God has unveiled something unique about who he is as he stands in relationship with a believing humankind.

That name, Jahweh, is constructed on the Hebrew verb meaning "to be." Thus Moses was told, "Say 'I AM' has sent you. If my people want to know my name—if they ask what my essential identity is—tell them, 'I AM.'"

What a stunning message!

You see, Israel in Moses' day had not experienced God as I AM. They viewed him as the great I WAS or the great I WILL BE. They knew that, ages before, God had been real to Abraham (I WAS). They thought that sometime in the distant future God might act again to keep his promises to Israel (I WILL BE). But they were not experiencing God as real in their present (I AM). Instead, all the Israelites were experiencing was the poverty of their existence as slaves. All they were experiencing—the focus of their reality—was the suffering burden of their oppression.

How like this our own experience can be! Eileen knows

all about the poverty of her existence. She knows all about the burden of suffering. As she waits for the unknown, Eileen is crushed by her present and drained of all hope for her future. As a Christian, she believes in Jesus as the Son of God who died for her (faith's great I WAS). As a Christian, she looks forward to a heaven in which her suffering will be ended (faith's confident I WILL BE). But burdened by the poverty of her present, Eileen has lost the vision of a God whose name is I AM!

For Israel, in Moses' day, God burst into history with unmistakable proof of his living presence. In quick succession, Egypt suffered ten searing, miraculous judgments that compelled Pharaoh to let God's people go. As the Israelites made their journey out of the land of oppression, God miraculously parted the sea for them, then closed the waters over Egypt's pursuing army. Every day the miraculous food (manna) supplied to them and the fiery-cloudy pillar that led their way gave Israel testimony to the vital, living presence of God. God acted. And a doubting people were suddenly confronted with the reality that God *IS*, that I AM is a God who is truly present with his people.

Sue, her time of waiting past, can testify to Eileen that God is still present, still active, still the great I AM. One day Eileen, too, will see God act in her life. When that time comes she'll know for herself what the Israel of Moses' day learned and what the Scriptures record to comfort us:

God sees the misery of his people.

God hears them crying out.

God is concerned about their suffering.

God comes down to rescue, to bring us to a good and spacious land.

God is still the I AM who can and will act in our present— still intimately, persistently, lovingly involved in our every today.

Even while we wait, God is.
Even while we suffer, God is.
And because God is the great I AM, not just the I WAS
or I WILL BE, you and I and Eileen can learn to practice
God's presence and discover the meaning of trust, even in
those times when we cannot believe.

"I'll tell you what helped me," Sue told Eileen. "It was
music. I go to an aerobic exercise group at our church,
and there were all these Christian songs we worked out
to. Not being into church music, I thought they were kind
of corny at first. But then I started really to listen to the
words: 'Free at last,' 'I'm Yours, Lord,' Songs like that. I
got tapes and began to play them at home. And the words
began to soak into my heart.

"We've got lots of tapes in our house now. My kids go
to sleep playing them. Whenever I'm down or discouraged,
God brings one of those songs to my mind, and I suddenly
remember just who he is and how much he loves me."

Practicing the presence of God means, first of all, finding
ways to remind ourselves of just who he is—ways of planting
deep in our consciousness the reality that, whatever our
present circumstances, God IS, and he is here with us.

For Sue, music helps.

For Debbie, who leads the exercise group at Sue's church,
it's memorizing Scripture. For Craig, a young neighbor who
comes weekly to our house for a singles' Bible study, it's
reading devotional books. For others it may be pictures
on the wall, Bible verses pinned on a mirror, Christian radio
listened to in the car. But for each of us, practicing the
presence of God means remembering that our God is I AM.
It means focusing on him and learning to see our circumstances in the light of his loving involvement.

It's important for us to affirm God's involvement in all
that happens to us. He is not just a passive observer. Just

as the Lord was involved in the centuries that Israel waited in Egyptian bondage, so he is involved in the months or years that we wait.

God is present and involved as we feel misery.

God is present, hearing each sob as we cry out.

God is present, deeply moved and concerned about our suffering.

And the God who is present will, in his own time, rescue us and bring us to a good land. Just as he rescued Israel from Egypt. Just as he rescued Sue from her lonely abandonment. Just as he will rescue Eileen from her desperate inadequacies.

The reality of a God who is I AM, always present with us, provides the basis for what Psalm 37 teaches us about trust.

"Be still before the Lord and wait patiently for him," Psalm 37:7 says. Waiting tends to create a sense of restlessness. Some are driven by it to frantic activity, hoping to block out the pain of their life's emptiness. But activity cannot help. What will help is to settle back into stillness, to learn patience. And the place in which we are to settle down is "before the Lord." We are to rest, facing him, gazing at his face, deeply aware as we gaze that God IS and that God is involved in our lives now, even though we are going through a time of waiting.

"Wait for the Lord and keep his way" (Ps. 37:34). This principle also echoes in verse 3: "trust in the Lord and do good." Our times of waiting and stillness are not to be times of inactivity. We are not to withdraw from life, but must wait for the Lord as our life moves on its normal, daily course.

Simply put, we are to do the good that each day puts before us. As Sue waited, she got up, dressed and fed her children, took them to a sitter as she hurried off to teach, came home, fed and played with the children, did her housework, corrected her papers, and fell exhausted into her empty, lonely bed. On Sunday she went to church, shared her feelings in her Sunday school class, and began to pray for her fellow singles as they shared with each other, found comfort in the truths the class studied and in her pastor's sermons, and came home to launch another week.

As Eileen waits, she, too, is learning to do good. She's learning to be responsible for her time. She's begun to take more care with her appearance. Seeing the gas credit card her husband left her as a symbol of her old dependency, she's stopped using it.

Eileen is still a long way from where she needs to be as a responsible, adult person. But she's learning to put her trust in the Lord into practice by doing good. She is learning that because God IS, and is present with her, the pain and the challenges of her waiting really can be faced, and her helplessness can be overcome.

"Commit your way to the Lord; trust in him, and he will do this" (Ps. 37:5). When we focus on God as a living presence who is with us today, we discover we can wait for tomorrow. We can let God establish the timing, the rhythm, the flow of life for us.

Oh, at times we still feel an urgency, and ache for our problems to be resolved once and for all. We may buy that occasional contest in the hopes that God plans to provide all the money we need instantly. We may send back the latest prize numbers Publisher's Clearing House has personally assigned to us and dream that our number will be the one God brings up. But increasingly as we focus on God as our I AM, we find we're willing to commit our way to him. We're willing to let him determine how to supply our needs. We're willing to trust him because we are confident that, in his own good time, he will act.

Making conscious, daily decisions to commit our way to God is helpful in practicing his presence. Doing this reminds us that we have a personal relationship with God—that not only does he speak to us, but we are also to speak to him. And it reminds us that when we speak, it is appropriate not only to ask him or to thank him but also to express our trust—to say to the Lord, "Father, I know that you are, and that you are with me. I commit today and my whole life to you. I trust your timing and your choice of the time when you will act."

How wonderful to have a God who is always present with us! How wonderful to have a God who cares so much that we can freely trust everything we are and have to him!

"The salvation of the righteous comes from the Lord; he is their stronghold in time of trouble" (Ps. 37:39). Our relationship with God is like a fortress. When troubles come, we hurry to him, and behind the massive walls and shuttered windows of his strength we know security. We wait for the Lord. But we also wait *in* the Lord.

When God's time comes, he will sally forth from his strong towers and by his actions win us our longed-for victory. But until then, however turbulent our days, we can rest—safe—in the God who is a stronghold in our time of trouble. We can wait patiently for him to act, to bring our time of trouble to an end.

The psalmist, David, who practiced God's presence faithfully for most of his long life, guides us in our own times of waiting by reminding us:

(1) *God truly is always present with us.* Whenever the name Jahweh occurs in the original Hebrew, our English versions mark its presence by capitalization: LORD. Each verse from Psalm 37 quoted in this chapter uses this deeply personal name, the name which calls our attention to God's essential nature as one always present with his people. We catch a glimpse of the wonder of this name as we paraphrase the key verses from Psalm 37:

Trust in God, who is with you this moment, and do good (v. 3).

Commit your way to the one who is with you even now; trust in him, and he will act (v. 5).

Be still before him who is ever with you, and wait patiently for him (v. 7).

Wait for the one who is with you, and keep his way (v. 34).

The salvation of the righteous comes from the God who is at their side each moment; he is their stronghold in time of trouble (v. 39).

The God of the Bible, the God you and I know in Jesus Christ, is no distant, disinterested figure whose attention is fixed solely on cosmic concerns. The God of the Bible, the God unveiled fully in Jesus, is a God of love who has committed himself to an intimate, constant, personal relationship with human beings. He is a God who is present with us now and will always be present. And it is because God truly is present with us that you and I can find trust by practicing his presence.

(2) *God needs only to be acknowledged to be experienced.* Just as David makes the Lord central in these verses from Psalm 37, so you and I can make the reality of God central in our awareness. We can do this by music, as Sue has done. We can do it by memorization or by reading or by meditation. However we choose to keep God in focus in our lives, remembering his presence does transform our experience.

The knowledge that God is with us gives us the courage to go on. The remembrance that God is beside us brings flashes of joy even in sorrow. The recall of God's presence comforts, strengthens, enables. Our experience of God during our waiting times may not be in an obvious miracle such as the ones that marked his presence in Moses' day. Instead, during our times of waiting the mark of God's presence is within. We sense him in the courage that enables us to take one more step. We recognize him in the joy that flashes unexpectedly in our unhappiness. We draw on his strength in our weakness. It is in these inner, hidden miracles that we experience in our most difficult hours that most of us discover the comforting presence of our God.

(3) *God's presence enables us to go on.* While we wait, we cannot withdraw from life. Human beings are not provided with some cave to hibernate in until life's winters pass. So, until God chooses to act, you and I must wait actively.

One of God's greatest gifts is that what we do while waiting is not meaningless. By committing each day to the Lord and doing the good that day's opportunities offer, we continue to "keep his way."

God's timing may not be the timing that we would choose. But we can always be assured that, even though his will is that we wait,

• God is ever present with us.
• God needs only to be acknowledged to be experienced.
• God's presence does enable us to go on.

For Meditation or Discussion

1. Can you think of inner, hidden miracles in your own life that were evidences to you of God's presence? In what circumstances did they appear?

2. Music is what helps Sue remember that God is one who is always present. What kinds of things have been, or do you think might be, helpful reminders for you?

3. Psalm 37's forty verses speak powerfully to the present experience of everyone who awaits God's timing. Read and meditate on this psalm, searching for the verses or phrases which best express: (a) some feature of your present experience, (b) a word of encouragement you need to hear, and (c) a word of guidance that points to what steps you should take next.

4

One of
These Days

Each of us experiences moments when we just can't wait any longer—when waiting hurts too much, or we become too discouraged. In those moments, we find it impossible simply to trust God's timing, and like Saul, we act foolishly.

What about these moments of failure? Do our foolish actions, our pressured sins, cut you and me off from God's blessing, as Saul's flawed faith cut him off from founding a royal dynasty?

For an answer to that question we need to look again at Saul—and at the man God turned to as Saul's replacement: David. The Bible calls David a "man after his [the Lord's] own heart" (1 Sam. 13:14). David was deeply aware of the Lord's presence and power, whereas Saul was consistently insensitive to spiritual realities. It's important to remember that Saul's foolish act in making a forbidden sacrifice was no isolated incident. It represents the basic attitude of this man, who started out with such promise, but whose inability to take spiritual truth into account generated so much tragedy. Saul's spiritual insensitivity was revealed again and again in other events in Saul's later life.

We see the contrast between Saul and David drawn sharply in a story every child knows. The sputtering feud of Israel with the Philistines flared up again one late spring.

The coastal peoples gathered their forces for war and assembled at Sucoh, in Judah. Saul gathered the Israelite forces to meet them. Like two bristling, growling dogs, the two armies faced each other, camped on opposite hillsides with a broad valley in between.

And there they waited.

They waited because of Goliath.

Often in ancient days battles were launched by heroes who met in individual combat before the general conflict. The Philistine champion was Goliath, a giant some nine feet tall, whose armor weighed one hundred twenty-five pounds and whose spear point weighed fifteen pounds. Each morning, Goliath marched out into the valley, shouted defiance, and dared Israel to send out a man to fight him.

But "Saul and all the Israelites were dismayed and terrified" (1 Sam. 17:11) by this huge warrior.

Saul, himself a head taller than the rest of his people, cowered in his tent and stared morosely into the valley, overwhelmed by the physical presence of the giant enemy.

And then David, a handsome but physically unimposing youth (see 1 Sam. 16:7), visited the army to bring bread and cheese to his older brothers. David naïvely wondered aloud why no one accepted Goliath's challenge—only to be angrily rebuked by his brothers. But David's words were reported to Saul who sent for him. And when standing before the king, David volunteered to fight Goliath.

Saul objected. "You're only a boy, and he has been a fighting man from his youth" (1 Sam. 17:33).

David's response shows us why this young man, destined to be king, was accepted by God as founder of a dynasty while Saul was rejected: "The Lord who delivered me from the paw of the lion and the paw of the bear will deliver me from the hand of this Philistine" (v. 37).

In facing this situation, Saul saw the giant.

David saw the Lord.

Saul was unable to see beyond the physical presence of his enemy. David was unable to understand how mere physical presence could matter in view of the real presence of God with his people.

Here is the critical issue for you and me as well. The person outside of God can sense only the material world and the physical realities of his or her situation. But you and I, like David, look beyond. We sense the God to whom creation mutely testifies. We recognize his work in history. And we come to know him in Jesus, acknowledging his love and welcoming his forgiveness. Like David, the tone of our lives has been set by faith. We have left the side of the cowering Saul to stand confidently beside the youthful shepherd boy who sees the Lord and who knows him so well.

But faith did not automatically release David from the agonies of waiting for God's timing. Nor will faith so release you and me. In fact, it sometimes seems that the more God loves, the more insistent he is that we take our place in his waiting room.

Even before the Goliath incident, Samuel had been sent to Bethlehem to anoint one of the sons of Jesse as Israel's next king. There God had pointed out the youngest of Jesse's sons, a boy whose outward appearance was ordinary but whose heart for God was exceptionally warm. And David had been anointed by the aging prophet. But years would pass, years filled with pressure and with waiting, before God's purpose would be fulfilled and David would be king.

Oh no. David's faith provided no release from waiting. Or from pain.

During the waiting years David did gain fame as one of Saul's generals. He won Saul's daughter as a wife. But finally Saul's jealousy drove David from the court. A few outcasts joined David as he lived in the wilderness as a fugitive. Towns David protected betrayed his presence to Saul, and armies of his own people pursued him as Saul determinedly sought to take his life. Harried and exhausted, David and his fellow outcasts struggled to stay alive in camps where hunger was no stranger.

David.

Born to be king.

But waiting, treated no better than some despised outlaw.

I understand the pressures of David's waiting years. Many a time, remembering David's forced wait has been a comfort to me.

I was converted and called to the ministry while in the Navy. After being discharged, I finished college and then spent four years in seminary, working full time to support my family while preparing for whatever ministry God chose. I expected to be a pastor. But then on graduation I was led to a Christian organization where my job was to write educational materials.

I didn't realize it at first, but I soon discovered that the job was my wilderness.

Unable to contribute because of the peculiarities of the person I worked for, I felt the pressures mount. It reached the point that every morning as I drove to work my stomach would knot with pain. Lunch hours were spent furiously pacing the streets to work off the day's fresh tensions. I struggled to find release, but again and again God confirmed my unwilling conclusion: His choice was for me to be there, blocked by the person I worked for from the ministering role to which I was sure God had called me.

As I struggled with my frustration and fought to remain submissive to my boss, I thought often of David. He, too, had a sense of God's call. He, too, fought to be submissive to the ruler God had appointed over him. He, too, was forced to wait, sure that God had a role for him, but blocked from fulfilling that role by forces beyond his control.

I thought of David, and I understood how tightly his stomach must have knotted. I thought of David, and I could visualize his furious marches. I could see him strike off, sometimes alone, to stride for miles in a vain attempt to release the mounting tension. I could share his agonizing times of prayer, times when he wept in frustration and cried out, "Why?"

You can understand too. You've known something of waiting's knotted stomach, of the tension that stretches you to the breaking point. You've known the struggle to keep on and the tearful prayers that bring no quick response.

And so you know that, under pressure, even men and women of faith may act foolishly—just as David did.

It was after another of faith's triumphs that David slipped. David and his forces, betrayed by neighboring villagers, were being pursued by Saul's army. Three thousand choice troops, led by Saul himself, had pushed David and his few hundred men out into the desert.

At night, David and several lieutenants stole back over the desert to look over Saul's camp. From a distance, David could make out Saul's resting place in the center of the camp, surrounded by his troops.

Impulsively, David decided to slip into the camp itself. He asked, "Who will go down into the camp with me to Saul?" (1 Sam. 26:6). Then, accompanied by Abishai, David left his stunned companions and picked his way through the sleeping soldiers.

In just a few moments David stood looking down at the sleeping Saul. Fiercely Abishai whispered to David, "God has delivered your enemy into your hands. Now let me pin him to the ground with one thrust of my spear!"

But David put a restraining hand on Abishai's arm. "Don't destroy him! Who can lay a hand on the Lord's anointed and be guiltless. . . . His time will come and he will die, or he will go into battle and perish. But the Lord forbid that I should lay a hand on the Lord's anointed."

So instead of striking Saul, David and Abishai slipped away with the spear and the water jug that lay by Saul's head.

Safely outside the camp, on a hill some distance away, David cried out to Saul. He showed the king his trophies and reminded Saul that despite the king's hostility, David had always acted as a loyal subject. Saul, momentarily ashamed, acknowledged David's righteousness and promised not to harm him. So David went on his way and Saul returned home.

It was then, in the moment of his triumph, that David made his mistake.

It often seems that the moment of our greatest danger is in our time of spiritual triumph. While I was attending the University of Michigan, I worked full time at a nearby state mental hospital. Each evening I conducted a Bible class for the men on my ward.

Quite a while after I had begun this practice, someone on the staff objected, and staff psychiatrists and the head nurse debated whether this practice was healthy for the patients. I was interviewed and questioned. Then the staff had to decide.

I had led the nightly class for nearly two years. During that time a number of men had received Christ, at least one suicide's family had been restored, and a good deal of spiritual comfort had been given to persons struggling in their own waiting rooms. A supportive chaplain had provided Bibles for all who wanted them, and I had been asked to preach in the chapel during his vacation. Now this little ministry was threatened. So I and others prayed that God would overcome the objections of the hostile and let the Bible class continue.

God did answer our prayer. Later, I heard that the hospital's chief administrator had settled the issue by telling several of the psychiatrists, "He ought to be holding a Bible class for *you!*"

And then, in the moment of triumph, I acted foolishly. Somehow, the victory won, I totally lost motivation. I became discouraged and found that I announced "class time" to my ward less and less frequently. Even when asked, "Will we have class tonight?", I found myself putting it off. My moment of spiritual triumph was also the moment of greatest vulnerability.

It was this way for David too.

In the moment of his spiritual triumph, he became most vulnerable. Just as I had, David suddenly found himself gripped by despair.

The story is told in 1 Samuel 27–29. Suddenly, with no apparent reason, this man of faith "thought to himself, 'One of these days I will be destroyed by the hand of Saul.'" Close to despair at the discouraging prospect, David acted foolishly and left Israel, deserting to the Philistines!

David took his six hundred men to Gath, one of five Philistine provinces, and pledged allegiance to Achish, the ruler of Gath. Achish, who knew of David's persecution by Saul, accepted David and gave David's men the border city of Ziklag to be their home. There David settled, in the land of his people's greatest enemies.

David's action did relieve the pressure from Saul, who gave up pursuit. But David's foolish choice involved him in a life of deceit—and in one terrible danger. From Ziklag, David raided peoples who were traditional enemies of Israel, taking their possessions but being careful to leave no survivors. When asked by Achish whom he had raided, David lied and said his attacks had been directed against settlements in the Negev, the southern deserts of Israel and Judah.

Achish smiled slyly at each report, smugly imagining that this renegade Hebrew was becoming so odious to his own people that he would be bound to Achish and the Philistines forever.

The danger came a year and four months after David settled in the land of his enemies.

Late spring once again brought the time of military campaigns, and the Philistines once more gathered their forces to fight against Israel. Achish said to David, "You must understand that you and your men will accompany me in the army."

Now David was trapped. Despite his earlier triumphs of faith, he had reached a point at which he could no longer wait, and he had acted foolishly. His uncharacteristic moment of despair had launched him on a course of action which took no account of God and was an overt rejection of God's call to continue waiting. And because David had acted foolishly instead of waiting, he was now in a position of having to fight against God's own people on the side of Israel's greatest enemy!

How tragic our hasty actions can be.

How much trouble we bring on ourselves when we decide that we cannot wait any longer, that it simply hurts too much to wait.

It's not that David didn't understand the issue. His own words show how clearly he recognized God's call to wait. Saul's "time will come," David had said to Abishai as they stood over the jealous ruler who had become David's enemy. "The Lord himself will strike him. . . . He will die, or he will go into battle and perish." But then, in a moment of despondency, David looked away from the Lord and muttered to himself, "One of these days I will be destroyed by the hand of Saul."

In that moment of uncharacteristic depression, a moment that followed immediately upon one of his great spiritual triumphs, David slipped. He acted foolishly, and his foolish action catapulted him into an impossible situation.

How like David each of us remains! We trust in God, and we, too, know the kind of triumphs faith won for David.

Yet we have times of depression, moments when we are vulnerable.

In our vulnerability, we, too, fail. Under pressure we sin— foolishly—convinced by the moment that we dare not continue to wait.

Invariably, our sins catapult us into impossible situations—situations over which we have no control.

What does life hold for us then?

Are we lost, having stepped beyond the boundaries of God's love? Are we rejected, objects now of God's anger rather than his concern?

Or is there hope for us when we, like David, have acted when God's timing demands we wait?

David's experience brings us comfort and hope. Fearfully, David led his six hundred to join the enemy thousands. How he must have struggled, torn within. He did not dare deny his allegiance to Achish; the Philistines would gladly have torn him and his men to pieces. But how could he actually fight against God's people, the very people he was one day to rule? It must have been with a fear-filled heart that David entered camp and reported to Achish.

But where David saw no solution, God had already been at work. The enemy commanders looked at this Jewish contingent marching with Achish. With angry suspicion, they confronted Achish with words to this effect: "Is this not David, the Hebrew who killed Goliath? Isn't he Saul's greatest general? How do we know he won't try to regain Saul's favor by turning on us in battle?"

Achish, confident of David's loyalty, defended him. But Achish was overruled. So Achish himself had to send David away, releasing him from the trap sprung by his own hasty action.

David played his role. He protested, acting out undeserved hurt. But deep within, David's heart must have sung! Ever sensitive to God, David must have realized that behind the Philistines' actions was God's own good hand.

God had not deserted David.

David had fallen, but God had reached down in love to snap the circumstantial chains David's sin had forged.

David was a man after God's own heart. But David, like you and me, was merely a human being, weak and fallible as the rest of mankind. Faith in God did not make David perfect or grant him relief from his temptations. But even in David's moments of unfaithfulness, God remained faithful to him.

This is something you and I can count on, too. Paul shouts it out in the New Testament—an exultant hymn of praise: "In all things God works for the good of those who love him, who have been called according to his purpose" (Rom. 8:28).

And Paul goes on, "He who did not spare his own Son, but gave him up for us all—how will he not also, along with him, graciously give us all things?" (v. 32).

And Paul adds even more: "I am convinced that neither death nor life, neither angels nor demons, neither the present nor the future, nor any powers, neither height nor depth, nor anything else in all creation, will be able to separate us from the love of God that is in Christ Jesus our Lord" (vv. 38–39).

God is able to take our hasty actions and by his hidden hand reshape our circumstances—or our hearts—to work his own great good. And God will do this for us even when we fail!

God has given us Jesus. With Jesus, and in Jesus, he graciously gives us all things.

How do our failures, our hasty sins and panicked errors, affect his attitude toward us? He continues to love. For nothing—nothing in this universe or beyond—can tear us away from God's enfolding love.

Saul and David were two very different men. Their lives took different paths; their decisions tended in different directions. Each was a man of great potential, and each had his character put to the test by a God who called on him to wait.

Saul could not wait even seven days. Under the pressure of his moment, Saul acted, and his action revealed the spiritual insensitivity which marked him all his days. All of Saul's crucial decisions reveal the same flaw that disqualified him from greatness.

David waited many years. He knew the persecution and the pain of misunderstanding. He waited out his decisive moments, strengthened by the confident trust that one day God would act. David's crucial decisions reveal a heart attuned to God, a sensitivity to the Lord expressed throughout David's life in obedience and in worship.

But David also knew times of failure—times the waiting hurt too much and he acted foolishly. But David's failures reveal only his natural human weakness and not a flaw in his relationship with God.

So it is with you and me.

What counts, what sets us beside David and apart from Saul, is our basic relationship with God through Jesus Christ. Once we have entered faith's door, have stepped across the threshold to accept the forgiveness purchased for us on Calvary's cross, we become members of the family of God. Our hearts become attuned to God and life takes on a direction like that of David's. The decisions you and

I make will tend more and more toward obedience, and our hearts will be more and more open to worship. Then, when we do fail—as fail we surely will—we can rest assured.

God redeemed David's foolish action.

God redeems our foolish actions, too.

God, who loves us as he loved this man after his own heart, will set us back again on the course he has planned for our life.

And often this means he will set us back where we were. Back on life's shelf. To wait.

But we can wait with confidence that remains unshaken even by our failures. In all things God is at work—at work for the good of those who love him. At work for your good. And for mine.

For Meditation or Discussion

1. If you were the author of this chapter, what guidelines would you draw from David's experience?

2. Think about the last few times you have been vulnerable and have acted foolishly. Can you see any patterns? What has been associated with your failures? What about times when you have been in similar circumstances and triumphed over the pressure or temptation? Can you describe anything in your past experiences which will help you live obediently in your moments of vulnerability?

3. Read and underline in your Bible the most significant words in Romans 8:28–39. Look particularly for thoughts that will help you sense God's continuing love for you, even when you fail him and yourself.

5

The Present Time

When Sue's husband left her, she wasn't the only one to suffer.

Their son, Pat, just turned three, felt the separation too. Pat would take paper sacks or his little canvas carrying case, pull the clothes out of his drawer, and pack them. Only later did Sue realize what Pat was doing. He was getting ready to leave. He was going to his father.

When this realization finally hit Sue, it hurt. Her husband, a rising executive in a large corporation, had never had much time for Pat. When diapers needed changing, it had always been, "Sue, will you get this kid changed?!" When Pat cried in the night, as he often did, his father would shake Sue and complain, "How can I get any sleep when he cries all night? Go pick him up!"

Sue's husband liked the idea of having children. He had a strong need to continue his line. But taking care of an infant or toddler wasn't his idea of a masculine duty.

So when Pat, hurt and confused by his father's abandonment of the family, showed how much he wanted to go to his dad, it hurt. It was Sue who had loved him through the stomach problems that had made him so demanding as a baby. It was Sue who had given herself to the point of exhaustion now that her husband had deserted them. It was Sue who had struggled to care for her two children, keep up the house, care for the yard, and meet all the bills on a third of the budget she'd had before. And now Pat, the son for whom she'd suffered so much, seemed to prefer his father. Now Pat, just like his dad, seemed ready to abandon her.

The next months and years were the most agonizing in Sue's life. Not just because she was waiting, trapped in one of those endless moments in which life seems to lack direction or goal or meaning. Those months were agonizing because Sue had to deal with the increasingly violent hostility of her young son.

One characteristic of our waiting times is that while we are waiting, we must continue to deal with present problems. We can't settle back, relax, and use the slack times of life as opportunities for rest. In fact, instead of giving us time to catch our breath, our waiting times seem to generate more pressures. Life is *more* harried, not less.

Sometimes when it hurts too much to wait we find our thoughts constantly drifting to the future. We dream about some sudden change that will set life in motion again. We imagine some unexpected inheritance. We project the healing of our illness. We fantasize a transformation in a loved one that will take away the hurt.

But somehow, we can't escape the present by dreaming of tomorrow. We are forced against our will to live through each today, to deal with today's pains, and to meet today's challenges.

It's encouraging at times like these to note a particular thread of teaching that runs delicately through the Scripture. J. B. Phillips, in his bold paraphrase of the the New Testament, picks up this thread in Romans 13:11, graphically rendering the verse this way: "the present time is of the utmost importance." The New International Version continues, "the hour has come for you to wake up from your slumber."

You and I can't live in our dreams. Even when life seems at a standstill and we are trapped in waiting, we must wake up and recognize that the present time is important.

Even if the present moment seems to have no purpose.

Even if the present moment is filled with anguish.

Even if it hurts too much to bear the pain a moment longer.

Even then, the present is important to God—and to you and me.

As Pat grew older, his actions showed how deeply troubled he was about his relationship with his dad. His father lived in the same city and saw the children frequently. But despite the afternoons and alternate weekends Pat spent with his father, his behavior at home became more and more hostile.

He loudly threatened that he would go live with his dad. He belittled his mother, contemptuously shouting, "What do you know?" when she'd talk with him. He began to abuse his little sister. He picked fights constantly, forcing unnecessary confrontations. In the morning he'd ask for Grape Nuts Flakes, and when Sue served the cereal he would shout angrily that he wouldn't eat that junk, he wanted Sugar Crisp. If Sue then got him the Sugar Crisp, he'd shout with angry tears that he didn't want that, he wanted Grape Nuts Flakes.

Pat's hostility came out in other ways, too. If Sue picked up a room, Pat would go in and scatter toys and papers. He'd use his toy scissors to rip gashes in the furniture, and his crayons to mark the walls. He'd run into his room, lock the door, and throw his clothes and bedding on the floor, shouting vulgar words and calling his mother names. He kicked a hole in one side of his door; he constantly left his bathroom filthy. Rejecting love and punishment alike, Pat seemed determined to live in open rebellion until somehow his own agonizing inner needs—needs no child could understand—were met.

What made this doubly hard for Sue was that she had met and was engaged to the man she would later marry. But despite the growing love and commitment between Sue and her fiancée, they couldn't be married for nearly a year. His weekly visits from out of town and the frequent phone calls only underlined the agony that waiting had become and the mounting futility Sue felt in dealing with her son. For Pat now lived in open, fierce rebellion against his mother, even though he seemed to respond to her fiancée.

The present in which Sue was forced to live was a searing anguish. Why had God insisted on this wait? Why hadn't he cleared the way for a marriage now, to give her release and to give her son a father? How could the present, with all its pain, be important, compared to the prospect of release that her future seemed to hold?

Sue did not know Isaiah's age-old promise. But she was about to experience it:

> Since ancient times no one has heard,
>   no ear has perceived,
> no eye has seen any God besides you,
>   who acts on behalf of those who wait for him.
> You come to the help of those who gladly do right,
>   who remember your ways (Isa. 64:4–5).

Secretly, where her eyes could not see and where no whisper of God's plan could reach her ears, God was at work, preparing to act for Sue and her son.

This is one of the two things that makes our present so important. *God's timing is a reflection of his hidden work.* Slowly, gradually, God shapes circumstances and prepares persons for their unique place in his solution to our problems.

Sue had experienced God's preparing work before. Before Sue and her former husband moved to the city where she now lives, Sue had come to know a very special neighbor. Elena was a teacher with two young sons. Elena had been abandoned by her husband and had struggled successfully to build a career in teaching, spend quality time with her boys, and care for their home. Elena had shared freely with Sue, and Sue had been deeply impressed by the faith and positive attitude of her neighbor. Later, when Sue had been jolted by the unexpected departure of her own husband, she had remembered Elena.

"If Elena can do it, so can I," Sue had muttered to herself as she struggled with her winter sidewalks. "If Elena can do it, so can I," Sue had thought as she forced herself out of bed in the morning to dress her children, take them to the babysitter, and make it to the school in which she was substituting that day.

Elena had been God's unexpected preparation for Sue's trial. God had been at work in a present that was now past, long before Sue's troubles came. God had given her Elena then as an encouraging gift, preparing her to face a future pain that he alone knew must come.

Our present is often like this. There are experiences, friendships, events that seem commonplace, but that are really God's preparation for our future. The present is of utmost importance because God is at work in every today, shaping us for our tomorrows.

As Sue now struggled to deal with Pat and with her own hurt and anger, she could not know what God was preparing. But he was at work.

Completely overwhelmed, Sue took Pat to a Christian counselor who had helped her through the first days of the desertion, a counselor who had become a close friend.

He talked with Pat, had Pat draw some pictures, and told Sue what they meant.

The most significant picture was Pat's drawing of a family. On one side of the page there was a crude representation of one large and one small person. On the other side was a featureless form, a blob. When asked to talk about the picture, Pat identified himself standing beside his father. He spoke vaguely of his sister. But not about his mother. He didn't want to talk about the blob or the great distance between them.

"Right now," the counselor told her, "Pat identifies completely with his father. His need for relationship with his dad is so strong that he can't deal with his relationship with you.

"What Pat needs is to go and live with his father."

To Sue it was the ultimate rejection.

Her husband had left her, abandoning her with the children. Now her son, whom she'd loved and cared for so unselfishly, wanted to abandon her, too—for her ex-husband!

She fought it.

She cried, thinking that if only the date for her marriage could be set forward, Pat would adjust. She could keep her son, and her new husband would help both of them through the crisis.

But the marriage date couldn't be set forward.

God's command of circumstances forced Sue and her fiancé to wait. To wait, when it hurt too much to wait. To wait, while Pat's behavior grew worse and worse and Sue could feel her self-control slipping away.

Sue's anger flared in response to Pat's hostility. Already sick and run down after three years of struggle, Sue's emotions surged, draining her of energy. Finally, afraid of what she might do to Pat if her control snapped, she faced the fact that she had to let Pat go.

It was January—grim and dark in Sue's chill Midwestern

state—when the three of them met to talk about Pat. Sue's fiancé explained to her ex-husband how desperate the situation had become. Her ex-husband, who had always thought that some day he would have his son, bargained. Would the change be permanent? Sue wouldn't change her mind, and want Pat back next week?

All three did look at what was best for Pat, and an agreement was reached. Pat would move in with his dad. By the next September, when Sue and her fiancé were married and all saw how Pat was doing, a final determination would be made.

And so, with a heart as bleak and dreary as the lowering clouds outside, Sue packed the belongings of her only, dearly loved son. She watched Pat's father carry his things out of her house, out of her child's room. She watched Pat smile as he settled down in the car beside his dad, smile as he waved goodbye and they drove away.

And she thought her heart would break.

"Oh God, why?"

"Why did we have to wait? Why couldn't we marry before this happened—before I lost my son?"

But there was only silence.

God did not speak to Sue.

And so the waiting continued. It was less pressured now because Sue's home was freed now of constant conflict with Pat. But the home was empty, too. Empty, except for the anguish with which Sue lived, the doubts and self-accusations, the hurt of a fresh abandonment which made her relive those terrible feelings of worthlessness which so often accompany divorce.

Often waiting is a time of darkening clouds. Our skies do not lighten. Instead, everything seems to become even more grim.

Yet the darkening of our skies may forecast the dawn.

It is in the gathering folds of deepening shadows that God's hidden work for us takes place. The present, no matter how painful, is of utmost importance.

Somewhere, where our eyes cannot see and our ears are unable to hear, God is. And God is at work.

There's a second thing about the present which makes it so important as we wait: *God is not only at work for us. God is at work in us.*

While Sue was going through her time of waiting, her present torment was serving as God's refining fire. Her faith was being tested and purified.

Each week Sue and her fiancé led a Bible study in her home. A small fellowship of singles gathered, shared, prayed, and struggled to grow in godliness. Sue shared her feelings and her fears, sensing the supportive prayers of her friends.

And Sue needed prayer.

Inside, Sue was fighting a fierce battle with herself. She fought against a mother's terror, struggling to surrender her young and tormented son to the Lord.

And Sue won.

She reached the place where she surrendered Pat to the Lord, telling God she was willing, if it was for her son's best, to have him live from now on with his dad. She told the Lord how afraid she was, but she also told him that she trusted him to know and to do what was best. And with that surrender came a sense of peace.

Pat was God's now.

Jesus, who always loved the little children, would surely do what was best.

The present time is of utmost importance because the pressures of waiting provide opportunities for us to grow. The present time—the time of pain, the endless wait—confronts us with our weakness and invites us to turn to God.

Learning to turn to God, to lean on him in total trust while we abandon our own efforts, gives an exciting meaning and purpose to our present. If you have been unable to see any good in your own waiting time, consider the good that God may intend to happen within you. Consider how waiting draws you closer to God, teaches you dependence, gives you time to struggle with your doubts and to achieve a deeper faith.

The present time is of utmost importance because *you* are important.

Not just what happens to you.

Not just your circumstances.

But you—your character, your heart—are vitally important to the Lord. And he uses present pain to scour and polish your soul so that you will shine with heightened glory in his presence.

One of Sue's favorite Bible verses reflects what she has learned about both aspects of her present:

> One thing God has spoken,
>   two things have I heard:
> that you, O God, are strong,
>   and that you, O Lord, are loving (Ps. 62:11).

Today, her waiting over, Sue is doubly convinced that God is both loving and strong.

When summer came, Pat missed his neighborhood friends. He missed sleeping in late; his dad had to rise early to go to work, and Pat had to go to the sitter's. He had visited at his mother's infrequently during the winter and spring. Now he was willing to move back there—"just for the summer."

Sue welcomed Pat back with mixed joy and fear. But Pat was changing. Being accepted by his father and living with him for those months seemed to have reassured Pat that when his dad had left his mother he wasn't divorcing *him.* That fear relieved, Pat was able to respond more positively to Sue, whom he no longer perceived as the cause of his dad's departure and an obstacle to Pat's living with his dad.

Then came fall—and the long-awaited marriage. Sue's new husband moved in with her little family. He loved them all, even the dog. Pat responded to his stepdad's discipline and to the exciting games the two played as his stepdad helped the first-grader with his reading and his math. When Pat's real father lost his local job and moved to another state, there was hardly a ripple. Some of Pat's things were moved with him, and Pat knew there would be visits there, that he would now have two homes where he was wanted and welcomed.

And suddenly, with the rebirth of love and the new marriage, Sue's waiting came to an end. The lonely nights were empty no longer. The vacant hours were filled. Sue's faith in God had been rewarded as the Lord once again showed himself to be both loving and strong.

Today, looking back, Sue can see the Lord's work in her forced wait. If she had remarried sooner, Pat would not have had those months with his dad that reassured him and released the pressures of his own fierce fears. If she had remarried sooner, Sue would not have known the joy of a triumphant faith that was fanned to brighter flame in those moments of her trial.

On the other hand, if Sue had remarried *later,* her exhusband might have been unwilling to let Pat return. The vital months of readjustment, complicated by a first year in school, would have passed without Pat's having the security he now finds in having another man at home.

Today, looking back, Sue can clearly see that God's timing was best. And she is awed as she remembers—awed by what God has done, awed by the miracles that to an outsider seem only lucky circumstances but that to eyes of faith display God's loving hand.

This is what our present promises each of us, even as we wait. The present is of utmost importance because God is at work *for* us—hidden to us, but at work still—preparing the good that will come. The present is of utmost importance because God is at work *in* us, refining our faith, teaching us that we can and must fully trust our Lord. The present is of utmost importance because today is God's pathway to tomorrow.

When tomorrow comes, then we will know for sure that God's pathway, though it lies in the shadows cast by long and painful waits, leads to joy.

So what do we need to remember as we live in our present, struggling to remember that it is an important time too?

(1) *God is at work in hidden ways during the present time.* Isaiah's promise is for you and me today:

> Since ancient times no one has heard,
>   no ear has perceived,
> no eye has seen any God besides you,
>   who acts on behalf of those who wait for him.
> You come to the help of those who gladly do right,
>   who remember your ways (Isa. 64:4–5).

God does exist. He does act on our behalf. You and I who wait for him, who gladly do right, will experience his coming to our aid.

Just what he is doing in our present to prepare for the moment of his action will usually be a secret, hidden from us and from others. But because we know the Lord and trust his love, we can wait. We do not wait hopelessly, though at times we may struggle with doubt. We wait, instead, hopefully. For him.

(2) *God's blessing of others is intended to encourage us.* Psalm 67 speaks of a day when "the land will yield its harvest, and God, our God, will bless us. God will bless us," the psalmist says, "and all the ends of the earth will fear him" (Ps. 67:6–7).

Looking back now, Sue is moved to wonder and awe at the blessings God has given her. Her story and the thousands of stories like it that can be told by God's people are meant to move our hearts to echo that wonder and awe.

How good God is! How loving, how powerful he is—how able to work in and through our darkest days and bring us to a bright tomorrow!

James underlines this same truth. "You have heard of Job's perseverance and have seen what the Lord finally brought about," he writes at the close of his letter. "The Lord is full of compassion and mercy" (James 5:11).

God's blessings come because he is so full of love for us. And every story of blessing reminds us of who he is, filling us afresh with awe, giving us renewed hope.

(3) *God wants us to take advantage of the opportunities of our present.* During waiting times, when we are filled with hurts, we may not realize that opportunity exists. But a unique opportunity is always there.

Waiting times seldom bring opportunities to *do.* Instead, they bring opportunities to *grow* and to *become.* When waiting, you and I have an opportunity to trust. We have an opportunity to pray. We have an opportunity to recognize our own weaknesses and express our trust in God.

The opportunities that waiting brings are opportunities to enlarge our hearts, to deepen our faith. The stiller waters of our lives may well run deep and call us to submerge

ourselves fully, abandoning ourselves to what we know of
God—

> That you, O God, are strong,
> and that you, O Lord, are loving (Ps. 62:11).

The present time *is* important:

- God is at work in your present—in hidden but very
  real ways.
- God's blessing of others can encourage you, calling
  you to remember with trusting awe his great compassion.
- And, God wants you to take advantage of your opportunities in the present, opportunities to deepen your personal relationship with the Lord.

For Meditation or Discussion

1. Looking back at past experiences, what stories of your
   own might illustrate God's determination to bless?

2. In what ways have you found your times of waiting to
   be opportunities for deepening your relationship with the
   Lord? How have you benefited from those opportunities?

3. Find one or two verses in the Psalms that encourage
   you to trust God while you wait. To help you, you might
   use a concordance, looking up the word *wait*. Or pick
   up the *Believer's Promise Book* (Grand Rapids, Michigan:
   Zondervan, 1984) at your library or Christian bookstore.
   Why do the verse or verses you chose seem to have
   special meaning for you?

6

Deeply Troubled

Hannah had reason to be bitter.

Elkanah, her husband, loved her better than he did his other wife, Peninnah. But Peninnah had children, and Hannah had none.

Children were viewed as a divine blessing in Old Testament times. A wife yearned to give sons and daughters to her husband, and especially to provide him with sons. Psalm 127's vivid imagery portrays the attitude of the Hebrews:

> Sons are a heritage from the Lord,
>   children a reward from him.
> Like arrows in the hands of a warrior
>   are sons born in one's youth.
> Blessed is the man
>   whose quiver is full of them (vv. 3–5).

The conscious decision not to have children that some people make today would have been unthinkable in Old Testament times. Then, children were central to life's meaning; a person's significance depended on the children who would carry on the family line.

So Hannah felt she had reason to be bitter. Though married for many years, Hannah had no children. She waited—

hoping, yearning, suffering—but no children came. Hannah's womb was closed; all that grew within her was a bitterness which wrapped its roots tighter and tighter around her soul.

It is during our times of waiting that we, too, are particularly vulnerable to becoming bitter. For waiting, which prepares the soil of our hearts for spiritual growth, also provides fertile soil for the noxious weeds of bitterness.

Hannah's story is told in the first chapter of 1 Samuel. The Bible's report is rich in insights and warnings, to help us when we, too, wait on God's timing and discover how deeply the waiting can hurt. Here is how Scripture tells the tale:

> Year after year this man [Elkanah] went up from his town to worship and sacrifice to the Lord Almighty at Shiloh, where Hophni and Phinehas, the two sons of Eli, were priests of the Lord. Whenever the day came for Elkanah to sacrifice, he would give portions of the meat to his wife Peninnah and to all her sons and daughters. But to Hannah he gave a double portion because he loved her, and the Lord had closed her womb. And because the Lord had closed her womb . . . her rival provoked her until she wept and would not eat. Elkanah her husband would say to her, "Hannah, why are you weeping? Why don't you eat? Why are you downhearted? Don't I mean more to you than ten sons?" (1 Sam. 1:3–8).

"To worship and sacrifice." Worship was a joyful experience in Israel. There were ecstatic songs and dancing; music and shouted praise. Several times each year, all of God's people were called together for a national worship experience. Family and friends met and talked and caught up on all the gossip. The rich smell of roasting meat, burned on the altar as sacrifice to the Lord, filled the air as the family groups camped in the fields around the Tabernacle, which held the ark of God and testified to his benevolent presence. Boiling cauldrons held the portions of the sacrifice that were set aside for the offerers—portions on which the worshipers would feast as they shared with their God the products of his blessings.

These were joy-filled times for Israel, and Elkanah looked forward to them eagerly. The sacred moments and the uplifting times of praise, enriched because shared with family and friends, were special to him, as to other godly Jews.

The women and children as well loved Israel's worship festivals. For boys and girls there was the excitement of the journey—running and playing with new friends, feasting on meat—and there was the sense of wonder that must have overflowed as they watched adults bow to Israel's God. How many stories the children had heard on the way to the festival—stories of God's help and power; of heroes like Joshua, like Deborah and Gideon, like Sampson, too.

For the mothers, festivals were times of reunion. They saw their families, many of whom resided in different towns. How good it was to have a chance to renew old bonds . . . and to show off their children.

"Can you imagine? How little Elihu's grown! Why, I'd hardly know him."

And, "Sarah! Why dear, you're getting prettier every year!"

And the crowning joy. "Mother, here's Jeremiah, your new grandson." Then everyone would gather around, just as folks do now, oh-ing and ah-ing over the newborn, commenting on his smile and the strong grip of his tiny hands, talking about just whose eyes he has, and just whose chin.

"Year after year," the Bible says, Elkanah "went up from his town to worship and sacrifice." Year after year he took his family—Hannah, Peninnah, "and all [Peninnah's] sons and daughters." Year after year Peninnah joyfully met her relatives, showing pride in all her sons and all her daughters.

But year after year Hannah, head held high to hide her shame, answered the same old question: "No, no children yet." Year after year she followed her husband, trudging up to the place of worship with a growing sense of despair, robbed by her barrenness of even the joy of worship.

It might not have been so hard if it hadn't been for Peninnah.

The Bible says that Hannah's rival "kept provoking her in order to irritate her."

We can imagine it now: Peninnah smiling at some compliment on her latest offspring, then glancing sidelong at Hannah as she says, "Oh, our husband, Elkanah, is such a virile man, isn't he, Hannah?" Peninnah asking Hannah to hold her toddler while she changes the new baby and saying with a smirk, "Oh, you're so lucky, Hannah. No babies for you to clean up." Peninnah, open at times in her ridicule, commenting, "I can't imagine why Elkanah keeps her around. Maybe just for housework; she's certainly worthless as a woman."

Under this kind of constant provocation, year after year, robbing her even of the consolation of the worship festivals, Hannah became bitter. And we can understand her bitterness. We might even empathize if Hannah felt, as well she might, that she had a *right* to be bitter.

Circumstances may well press in on you and me too. Cary's wife, unresponsive and distant during the first years of their marriage, has cut herself off from him physically as well as emotionally these last eight years. He tries to live lovingly with her. But recently she's begun to attack him bitterly, telling all sorts of stories to their church friends and even their children.

Yvonne has been married for fifteen years. Although she desperately wants children, the years have brought nothing but three miscarriages.

Al had hoped to be a lawyer. He has a good mind, a

commanding presence, and a way with words that's made him a popular speaker at his lodge. But Al's years in the army, followed by an accident when he fell off a dam fishing, kept him from achieving his dream. For thirty years he's been a rural mail carrier, trapped in a routine that pays his bills but is empty of intellectual challenge.

You can think of others—others who like Hannah, like Cary, like Yvonne, and like Al might well argue that they have a right to be bitter. The circumstances of each of their lives are difficult. Each is trapped in a situation in which he or she can only wait.

But when human beings are trapped in difficult circumstances, do we really have the right to bitterness? Or is a phrase in 1 Samuel 1 for us as well as Hannah? She had no children. But the Bible says, twice in these few verses, that she was childless because "the Lord had closed her womb."

God, the loving Father we know so intimately in Jesus, was himself responsible for Hannah's circumstances. God had made his choice, and God's choice for Hannah involved years of anguish, years of pain-filled "wait."

When you and I sense God behind the circumstances of our lives, it becomes harder to justify a reaction like bitterness. In fact, just the bare *possibility* of God's involvement in our circumstances ought to give us pause. If this is God's choice for us, is it possible that he intends some hidden good? If this is God's choice, shouldn't we remain open to his purpose rather than closing our hearts and, in the chill darkness, letting the weed of bitterness grow?

Hannah's situation was not even totally bleak. Oh, we can understand the pain she felt and the constant irritation caused by Peninnah's pride. To have this go on, year after year, would stretch any of us to the breaking point.

But Hannah was not alone. She had a husband who loved her. Elkanah even showed his favor openly, giving her a double portion at the sacrificial meal and comforting her when she wept. We can see Elkanah now, sitting down beside his heartbroken wife, slipping his arm around her shoulder while he gently tells her how much he loves her. "Why," he says with a smile, "Don't I mean more to you than ten sons?"

But neither Elkanah's love nor his little jokes can reach the angrily despondent Hannah.

This is one of the terrible things about bitterness—it so fills our hearts that there is no room for enjoyment of our blessings. Bitterness distorts our vision, and we just can't see the good things that are intended to remind us of God's care. Elkanah's constant love might have encouraged Hannah and made her thankful. She might have remembered in her pain that the same Lord who had closed her womb had given her a loving husband. But in her bitterness Hannah simply could not focus on the good in her life.

There are good things in every life, even when we are stalked by tragedy. Cary's marriage is a constant source of pain, but he has a close relationship with his children. Yvonne has no children but, like Hannah, has a husband who loves her deeply. Al's career dreams will not be fulfilled, but he is loved by his family and highly respected by hundreds in his lodge.

If you and I can only tear away the thick vines of bitterness that have overgrown the windows of our soul, we can look out and see the many blessings that God gives. And the vision of blessings can fill us with a comfort that concentration on tragedy denies.

But the Bible's rendition of Hannah's story continues:

Once when they had finished eating and drinking in Shiloh, Hannah stood up. Now Eli the priest was sitting on a chair by the doorpost of the Lord's temple. In bitterness of soul

Hannah wept much and prayed to the Lord. And she made a vow, saying, "O Lord Almighty, if you will only look upon your servant's misery and remember me, and not forget your servant but give her a son, then I will give him to the Lord for all the days of his life, and no razor will ever be used on his head." As she kept on praying to the Lord, Eli observed her mouth. Hannah was praying in her heart, and her lips were moving but her voice was not heard. Eli thought she was drunk, and said to her, "How long will you keep on getting drunk? Get rid of your wine."

"Not so, my Lord," Hannah replied. "I am a woman who is deeply troubled. I have not been drinking wine or beer; I was pouring out my soul to the Lord. . . . I have been praying here out of my great anguish and grief" (1 Sam. 1:9–16).

Bitterness of soul can surely bring us to tears. But bitterness may also bring us to prayer.

This is one of the benefits of the waits that God sometimes imposes on us. Our times of waiting may bring us anguish and grief. But they may also provide us with a new perspective.

This seems to be what had happened to Hannah. For years Hannah had desperately desired a child. She wanted a son to give to her husband. She wanted a child to satisfy her own needs. She wanted a child to silence the taunts of her rival, Peninnah. Each was a valid reason; each motive was deeply felt. But finally, when the bitterness became so great that life held no more joy, when all that Hannah knew was anguish and grief, she found another reason to desire a son.

She wanted a son to give to the Lord.

Now, there surely was some selfishness in this desire. Hannah was bargaining with God. But the desire that her son might be someone God could use in a special way was something new. Somehow there had been a reordering of

Hannah's priorities, a new way of looking at what might give life meaning.

Out of Hannah's anguish and grief a new priority was born, and she offered to give God first place in her life, even surrendering to the Lord the son she yearned for so desperately.

The next morning, the Bible tells us, the family arose and worshiped before the Lord, then went back to their home. There, "in the course of time," Hannah conceived and bore a son. She named that son Samuel. And after Samuel was weaned, Hannah kept her promise; she dedicated Samuel to serve God as an apprentice of Eli's at Israel's worship center at Shiloh.

As the years passed, Samuel grew to be one of history's most faithful spiritual leaders, a man who guided Israel through the last days of the judges and into the establishment of the monarchy. As the years passed and Hannah witnessed the way that God was using her growing son, how glad she must have been. How she must have thanked the Lord, even for her years of pain, now that time had revealed something of God's good purpose.

The Bible tells us that Hannah continued to be blessed. "The Lord was gracious to Hannah; she conceived and gave birth to three sons and two daughters. Meanwhile, the boy Samuel grew up in the presence of the Lord" (1 Sam. 2:21).

There's a vital lesson for us in Hannah's experience. When bitterness drives us to anguish and grief, it may be time for you and me to reexamine our priorities. The anguish and grief may be divinely engraved invitations to turn to God in prayer and to explore the motives that lie behind our fierce desires. It may be that we need to know a change in motivation like that Hannah experienced. It may be that the area of our lives in which we remain so troubled needs to be abandoned more fully to him.

But beyond this lesson, there is also a promise: You and

I cannot outgive God. Hannah gave one child to the Lord. And God gave five times as much to Hannah—without even taking Samuel away. Hannah saw Samuel grow up. She sewed his clothing, spent time with him when the family came to worship. And Hannah had the wonderful knowledge that her boy was growing up in intimate relationship with the Lord.

Whatever we surrender to God when we reorder our priorities is not lost, but found. Whatever we give, we receive back multiplied.

What do we learn from Hannah about the bitterness to which each of us is so vulnerable in our time of waiting?

(1) *God remains the one behind our circumstances*. The Lord was the one who had closed Hannah's womb. And he could have changed Hannah's circumstances sooner. He could have changed the situations in which Cary and Yvonne and Al lived. He could change our situation, too, when you and I hurt and wait. But God has a purpose in our pain, and his purposes are always good.

Hebrews invites us to look at our times of waiting as moments of discipline—as training, not as punishment. "Our fathers disciplined us for a little while as they thought best," the writer says. "But God disciplines us for our good that we may share in his holiness. No discipline seems pleasant at the time, but painful. Later on, however, it produces a harvest of righteousness and peace for those who have been trained by it." Then the writer goes on: "Therefore, strengthen your feeble arms and weak knees" (Heb. 12:10–12). When we sense God's hand in our trials and remember that his purposes are always good, we'll find the strength to keep on despite the pain.

But then we have the warning. As we wait we are to "make every effort to live in peace with all men and to be holy." We are to "see to it that no one misses the grace of God and that no bitter root grows up to cause trouble and defile many" (Heb. 12:14–15). While we wait for God to act, we are to go on with our lives, living through each day as best we can. And we are to beware that bitterness can distort our lives and the lives of others.

Only a vision of God and the confidence that his purposes for us are good can guard us from bitterness's evil root. Only acknowledging him as the cause behind the other causes of our misery can free us to go on.

(2) *God provides constant reminders of his grace.* Even when the pain is greatest, we are not left without evidence of God's love. For Hannah it was a loving husband, Elkanah, who refused to reject her even though she had no children. His tender concern was a constant witness to God's own great, deeply personal love.

It's all too easy for you and me, when bitterness stirs, to focus on the Peninnahs in our life and to overlook the Elkanahs. God wants us to look instead at the positive, to seek out and to acknowledge the evidences of God's grace that always surround us.

Hannah had her husband. She had opportunities for worship. She had her material needs met.

You and I have friends or loved ones, too. We have those who care, as well as those who try to provoke us. We, too, have days set aside to worship and thank God. We have believing companions who can encourage us if we will but share our needs.

If we look for the blessings in our life and make them the basis for praise, we'll not miss the grace of God. Bitterness will find no place to take root in our lives.

(3) *God invites us to examine our priorities.* Even though waiting and its pain are not punishment, they may be discipline. They may be God's call to a holiness we have not

yet experienced, to a fresh insight into how our lives can be more fully linked to the Lord.

Our motives, like Hannah's, may need to undergo change. Our plans, like Hannah's, may need redirection. Our hopes, like Hannah's, perhaps too selfish, may need fresh recommitment to the Lord.

This isn't always the case. But waiting and waiting's pain give each of us an opportunity for self-examination. That self-examination may well reset the direction of our lives, guiding us to the place where God's richest blessing lies.

So, when waiting turns bitter, we do know how to respond:

- We remember that God remains the one behind our circumstances.
- We look around, sensitive to the evidence of his ever-present grace.
- And we reevaluate our lives, ready to reset our priorities to match what we know of his own.

And then there comes a release from bitterness. Then we find peace, even as we continue to wait. Then, in God's own time, we'll find the rich blessings that God has scattered there for us to find at the end of even the longest, most painful wait.

For Meditation or Discussion

1. Reread the story of Hannah in 1 Samuel 1. What lessons do you see for a person whose waiting is turning him or her bitter?

2. What are the most terrible effects of bitterness? How does bitterness affect a person and his or her

relationships? How have the times when you've felt bitter affected you?

3. What do you see in your life right now that gives indication of God's grace? How is God showing you his continuing love?

7

In Vain

Bitterness has a twin.

Jealousy.

In our long hours of waiting on God's timing, you and I are particularly vulnerable to both.

One great value of the Psalms is that the writers freely share their emotions. We're invited into the hearts, into the deepest thoughts and feelings, of persons who struggled with the same issues that trouble you and me.

In one of the Bible's most emotional and revealing psalms, we share the experience of Asaph, a man called on by God to wait, and a man who "almost slipped" under the pressure of jealousy.

If your waiting has ever generated the slightest twinge of jealousy, much less the burning ache that consumes hope, then Psalm 73 has a very special message for you.

The psalm begins with Asaph's confession. Then it moves on to describe his external circumstances, examine his frustration and personal restraint, and describe the key he found to recovering perspective. Finally, the psalm concludes with an affirmation of a wonderful reality that can protect you and me when our times of waiting make us vulnerable to jealousy.

Asaph's confession is a simple one. He knows that God

is good to his people. But he confesses that he almost lost his spiritual footing when he was gripped by envy:

> Surely God is good to Israel,
>   to those who are pure in heart.
> But as for me, my feet had almost slipped;
>   I had nearly lost my foothold.
> For I envied the arrogant
>   when I saw the prosperity of the wicked (Ps. 73:1–3).

The Hebrew word translated here as "envy" is also translated in some English versions as "jealousy." The basic meaning of the original portrays an extremely strong emotion, a burning desire. Whenever such a desire is focused on something not rightfully ours, it is wrong.

The New Testament almost always casts jealousy and envy in the negative (except 2 Cor. 11:2). This is because jealousy and envy tend to erupt in hostile acts (see Acts 5:17–18, 13:45, 17:5). Thus, jealousy finds a prominent place in the New Testament's lists of those kinds of behavior which spring from humanity's fallen nature. Envy and jealousy are associated with "outbursts of anger" (2 Cor. 12:20; Gal. 5:20) and interpersonal strife (Rom. 13:3; 1 Cor. 3:3).

Waiting is apt to find you and me looking longingly at the situations of others. When we do, we're vulnerable to desiring what they have rather than being satisfied with what God has given us. As jealousy grows, we may keep it locked up for a time, but ultimately it will spill over into angry conflict.

You and I realize that God is good to the pure in heart. But we, like Asaph, may lose our spiritual foothold when we see the prosperity of others and sense the crushing weight of our own relative poverty.

And it is not just financial poverty that creates our jealousy; it is the apparent poverty of our whole lives, measured

by whatever standard is meaningful to us at the time—
health, success, even release from the anguish of the waiting.

Asaph describes the persons whose success most troubled
him. They were the "beautiful people" of his world—those
whose sins and excesses the masses admired. He envied the
"arrogant," who seemed to have no troubles despite their
contempt for God. Asaph wrote:

> They have no struggles;
>   their bodies are healthy and strong.
> They are free from the burdens common to man;
>   they are not plagued by human ills.
> Therefore pride is their necklace;
>   they clothe themselves with violence.
> From their callous hearts comes iniquity;
>   the evil conceits of their minds know no limits.
> They scoff, and speak with malice;
>   in their arrogance they threaten oppression.
> Their mouths lay claim to heaven,
>   and their tongues take possession of the earth.
> Therefore their people turn to them
>   and drink up waters in abundance.
> They say, "How can God know?
>   Does God the Most High have knowledge?"
> This is what the wicked are like—
>   always carefree, they increase in wealth (Ps. 73:4–12).

For Sue, it wasn't her son Pat's rejection that hurt most.
What hurt most was that he seemed to prefer her ex-husband. Her ex-husband, who'd always been too busy to give
their toddler time. Her ex-husband, who'd left her alone
and pregnant, struggling financially, emotionally and physically drained.

This is one of the frightening things about our own times
of forced waiting. We see others who are so much better
off—others who seem "free from the burdens common to

man" while we are trapped in an endless struggle. All too often we can't even console ourselves with the thought, "Well, they deserve every good thing." Too often it seems to us that what they deserve is punishment, not blessing.

It certainly seemed to Sue that her ex-husband did not deserve the loyalty and love of their son, a loyalty and a love that for a time were denied to her.

It is at times like these that jealousy flares. We compare our situation with that of the undeserving other who seems so well off, and we begin to brood. The frustration can easily lead to despair.

Asaph captures his thoughts and feelings powerfully:

> Surely in vain have I kept my heart pure;
>   in vain have I washed my hands in innocence.
> All day long I have been plagued;
>   I have been punished every morning (Ps. 73:13–14).

It as at times like these that waiting may hurt the most. "God is good to those who are pure in heart." This keystone of Asaph's faith was expressed in the first verse of his psalm. But when Asaph sees the prosperity of the wicked and the poverty of his own present experience, he begins to doubt. "Surely in vain have I kept my heart pure."

Asaph has not let his feelings pressure him into foolish actions or hasty sins. Asaph has waited for the Lord, and kept on doing good. Despite the pressures, Asaph has kept his heart pure.

But God hasn't done his part.

God hasn't responded by being good to him!

At least that's the way it feels to Asaph.

This is a way of thinking that you and I are terribly vulnerable to as our waits on God's timing stretch into months and years.

Hannah thought, "I've got a right to be bitter." You or I may never fall into that trap. But we are all likely to begin to doubt. We're all likely to wonder why God has forgotten us. God is good to the pure in heart. And we've struggled to keep our hearts pure. Why then isn't God good to us?

If our doubts coincide with some experience that brings us face to face with the relative prosperity of those we know are wicked, the temptation is almost unbearable. Frustrated, despondent, we begin to feel with Asaph, "What's the use?"

"Why should I keep trying? I've worked so hard, and then *she* got the promotion!"

"What's the use? Helen's husband took her to Hawaii for a vacation, and she never even cleans the house. I work to keep our home spotless, and Herb never even notices when I polish or vacuum."

"I've worked for years in our Sunday school. But when they pick a Vacation Bible School director, they never think of me."

"I'm a trained teacher. How come no one thought of me for the Christian Education board—and put *him* on instead? Why, he doesn't know the first thing about education!"

You and I may find satisfaction in the knowledge that we are doing our best. But when others, less deserving, receive the promotion or the raise or gain the recognition—it hurts. Then, with Asaph, we begin to compare our efforts with theirs, and we begin to feel discouraged. What's the use? "In vain have I kept my heart pure." God, who is "good to the pure in heart" seems to have reserved his best gifts for the undeserving and to have forgotten us.

We don't know how long Asaph was trapped by his feelings of jealousy and his conviction that God was unfair. But we do know that Asaph, one of Israel's worship leaders, struggled to resolve his feelings while remaining true to his calling:

If I had said, "I will speak thus,"
I would have betrayed this generation of your children (Ps. 73:15).

Often our feelings are in conflict with our knowledge. We *know* that God is good, whatever may happen to us. We are intellectually convinced that he is fair and are sure that he loves us. But we still *feel* betrayed. The pain is still there; the frustration still sends out tendrils of doubt.

In such a situation many of us may find the strength Asaph found. He refused to speak his doubt publicly; he continued to teach what he knew must be the truth about God. He would not let his personal pain lead him to betray others who trusted him to represent the Lord.

But although you and I may continue in our hurt to share what we know about God and not let God's truth be distorted by our emotions, we still must face the inner struggle. Asaph says:

When I tried to understand all this,
it was oppressive to me (Ps. 73:16).

Asaph struggled. But he could find no key to unchain him from his jealousy and doubt.

And then he found a key! It's a key that may unlock and free us as well from our chains of jealousy and doubt. Asaph's key was to take God's view of time, to measure reality not by the present moment, but by life's destiny.

Trying to understand was oppressive to Asaph,

till I entered the sanctuary of God;
then I understood their final destiny.
Surely you place them on slippery ground;
you cast them down to ruin.
How suddenly are they destroyed,
completely swept away by terrors!
As a dream when one awakes,

so when you arise, O Lord, you will despise
them as fantasies (Ps. 73:17–20).

It's important not to miss the psalmist's point here. It
isn't simply that the wicked will be destroyed in the end.
The point is that what Asaph had taken as an indication
of God's blessing on the wicked was really evidence of the
Lord's anger! In giving these people no struggles, in freeing
them "from the burdens common to man," God had actually
placed them "on slippery ground!"

In their prosperity, the wicked imagine that they have
no need for God.

In our struggles, in our enforced waits, you and I have
no such illusion.

It's strange, isn't it? God is good to the pure in heart.
But God's idea of goodness may not fit our notions of blessing. God's good for you and me may be suffering. It may
be illness. It may be financial strain or heartbreak. God's
good for the pure in heart is anything that draws us close
to him and prepares us for the final destiny of his saints.

The things that we tend to look at as good—the material
blessings, the life of ease—are slippery ground for human
beings. Those who wander there, never forced to wait on
God's timing until it hurts too much to wait, will waken
one day to find their "good" a dream. Then the character
of the pure in heart, forged in faith's enforced wait, will
be found to be what is real.

Asaph's sudden insight transformed his perspective and
drove the jealousy from his heart. He writes,

When my heart was grieved
and my spirit embittered,
I was senseless and ignorant;
I was a brute beast before you (Ps. 73:21–22).

Asaph recognized his thoughts and feelings of jealousy
for what they were. They were senseless—the instinctive

reaction of an animal to danger and to pain, the instinctive reaction of a being whose perceptions are limited to this universe and who has no access to the realities beyond.

But you and I, like Asaph, can look beyond the confines of this material universe and discover the spiritual realities beyond. We can even understand the principles on which God orders our experiences—and find his way to live while waiting. In his last verses, Asaph gives us significant insights which not only help us overcome jealousy, but also show us how to live triumphantly when we are forced to wait:

> Yet I am always with you;
>   you hold me by my right hand.
> You guide me with your counsel,
>   and afterward you will take me into glory.
> Whom have I in heaven but you?
>   And being with you, I desire nothing on earth.
> My flesh and my heart may fail,
>   but God is the strength of my heart and my portion forever
> (Ps. 73:23–26).

Asaph's solution is penetrating in its simplicity. He says to recognize the presence of God ("I am always with you"). He says to take each step as God guides us ("You guide me with your counsel"). And he says to be satisfied with the Lord ("being with you, I desire nothing on earth").

God *is* with us, always. He shows us the path ahead of us—one step at a time. We don't know what next month, or next year, or the next decade will hold. But we do know that, as we live life one step at a time, God's counsel will lead us to glory.

In the meanwhile, we are to be satisfied with the Lord. There's nothing on earth that can compare in significance with knowing him. When we have the Lord and have him ever with us, we have everything.

How good to know that God, our God, "is the strength of my heart and my portion forever."

Asaph's last two verses sum up what he has learned through his experience. These verses invite us, too, to pause and think. What does God want you and me to learn through our waiting? What does he want us to learn from the jealous envy that may tug at our hearts? If we make the same discovery that Asaph made and reach the same conclusions, then our long waits are blessings indeed.

> Those who are far from you will perish;
> you destroy all who are unfaithful to you.
> But as for me, it is good to be near God.
> I have made the Sovereign Lord my refuge;
> I will tell of all your deeds (Ps. 73:27–28).

Among the many lessons that we learn from this psalm, which seem to be most significant for those who wait? Perhaps these:

(1) *God's blessings are often disguised as pain.* We can be convinced that God is "good to the pure in heart." But unless we recognize the nature of his "good," we may be trapped into jealousy.

Asaph mistook material prosperity to be an unmixed "good." The setbacks he suffered were "bad" because they caused him pain. But in making this evaluation, Asaph later acknowledged, he was reasoning in a "senseless and ignorant" way. When Asaph recovered his spiritual awareness, he realized how foolish this notion was. He saw that what feels good for a time is not "the good" for human beings, for each individual's destiny stretches beyond time into eternity. Asaph saw that those whose lives are without difficulty tend to discount God, feeling in their pride that they can get along very well without him.

On the other hand, Asaph's agonizing wait had driven him to the Lord. Asaph was forced by his troubles to discover the sufficiency of God.

Thus, what Asaph experienced as "bad"—the illness, the poverty, the plague of human ills—was actually God's "good" gift to him!

You and I are deeply loved by God. Like Asaph, we may suffer. But, also like Asaph, you and I have the assurance that God *is* good "to those who are pure in heart." When we grasp this reality, our attitudes will be transformed, and we will sense the presence of the Lord in our trials.

(2) *God's purposes often focus beyond the range of our vision.* We live in a "bottom line" society. We want results, and we want to see them *now.* We want to look at the short-term profit and loss. We want the solution provided in the span of a two-hour movie in which the good guy gets the girl and the bad guy is crushed in fantasy's Temple of Doom.

But God's sense of timing and his purpose differ from our own, just as his sense of values differs. You and I complain, "all the day long I have been plagued," unaware that to God a day is a thousand years and a thousand years an instant. If life itself is as fleeting as a dream, and we will awaken to eternity, how can we complain of divine mistreatment? We have not even begun to sense the glory that God has in store for those who love him.

Unlike the wicked, who will suddenly be swept away in terrors, you and I will awaken to joy. God will call, this life's brief day will end, and then we'll know for all eternity the rich store of good that God treasures up for the pure in heart.

Normally the glory that follows our long waits comes partially in this life. Just as in the case of Sue, whose dark years of desertion led to the brightness of a fresh love, our dark clouds will also disappear. In this life as in the next we'll experience the rich blessing of God. But we need to be careful while we wait. God's "standard time" is not our own. The strain of what seems to us too long a wait may well be, to him, a rushing flow that bears us on to a blessing we'll discover tomorrow.

(3) *God's presence comforts and sustains.* While we wait, we need to fix our eyes on the Lord. To look away, to compare ourselves with others or to gaze enviously at this world's goods, brings only misery.

God has not called us to jealousy, but to satisfaction and to peace.

We can find that satisfaction, now, in him. He holds our hand. He guides us day by day. Having him, our portion forever, we are released from harmful desire.

Yes, jealousy and envy are invitations. They are God's call to us to remember:

- God's blessings are often disguised as pain.
- God's purposes are focused beyond the range of our vision.
- But through it all, God's presence comforts and sustains.

For Meditation or Discussion

1. What is the most important lesson that you draw from Psalm 73? Why is this lesson so important to you?

2. How has your spiritual experience been affected by prosperity? During times when you have experienced this world's "good," have you been closer to or more distant

from the Lord? Do you have any insights into the "why" of your experience?

3. Who or what are you most likely to envy? When you sense envy springing up in your heart, how do you think you will respond in the future?

8

Hope

When Sue told Eileen on the phone that her future would be better, Eileen could only think, "That's all right for you to say. You have a husband."

Somehow when you and I are hurting, "positive thinking" holds very little attraction. Waiting brings discouragement and often despondency. If this is how you respond when it hurts too much to wait—not by hasty actions, but by oversleeping, by lethargy, by slipping into depression—then God's antidote may be an infusion of hope.

Hope is a slippery word in English. We use it to express the most adolescent, wildly optimistic notions: "I hope to become a movie star and make millions of dollars." And we also use it to express hesitant doubt: "I hope I can do the job, but it looks awfully hard." With such widely ranging meanings, we need to understand the biblical meaning of hope as something you and I can experience in our times of special need.

When we do look into the Bible, we find that the Old Testament and New Testament use *hope* with significantly different emphases.

---
*This chapter is an adaptation of the author's study of "hope" in the *Richard's Expository Dictionary* (Grand Rapids, Mich.: Zondervan Publishing House, 1985).

There are two Hebrew words translated "hope" in our English versions of the Old Testament. One is *miqᵉweh,* or *tiqᵉwah* (variant spellings of the same word). The other is *yahal*. Each of these Hebrew words breathes confidence; each invites us to look ahead eagerly. There is no uncertainty here, no doubtful hesitancy. But there is patience. There is an awareness that the fulfillment of our brightest hope lies in the future.

Of the two, the *qᵉweh*-word encourages us to look ahead. Job, in what is perhaps the oldest book in our Bible, selected this word when he was catapulted into his own long and agonizing wait.

Job had become comfortable in his relationship with God. And Job had been blessed. He had been rich not only in goods, but also in children and in merited respect. But in a single day, Job lost his possessions, his family, and his health. And the friends to whom he might have looked for comfort took the role of accusers. "God wouldn't have let this happen," they argued, "if you weren't guilty of some hidden sin."

Job, stunned by what seemed to him a divine betrayal as well as anguished by the harshness of his friends, was close to despair. "If the only home I hope for is the grave," he complains, ". . . where then is my hope?" (Job 17:13–15). But although Job faced a fearful future, he rejected the suggestion of Eliphaz: "Should not your piety be your confidence, and your blameless ways your hope?" (Job 4:6).

Job was sure that his suffering was not punishment for sin. But Job would not base his hope for the future on his own supposed sinlessness. Ultimately, Job found in God a foundation for hope, as did the psalmist: "Lord, what do I look for? My hope is in you" (Ps. 39:7).

This is the Old Testament's basic answer to our questions about the future: Don't have hope because of confidence in yourself. Don't be afraid because of the dark circumstances of your life. Look to God, and hope in him.

According to Scripture, Israel's confidence in God was founded on his covenant. A covenant, in its simplist meaning, is a contract, a commitment by which one or more parties bind themselves to do certain things. God had appeared to Abraham, and while Abraham simply watched, God had made an unbreakable compact with this man and his descendants (Gen. 15). God's commitment was to bless, not harm, this people.

Everyone who lives in personal relationship with God can count on this same commitment. God has promised. He intends to bless us. And that intention can never be shaken.

The writer of the New Testament Book of Hebrews later picked up this same theme:

> Because God wanted to make the unchanging nature of his purpose very clear to the heirs of what was promised, he confirmed it with an oath. God did this so that, by two unchangeable things in which it is impossible for God to lie, we who have fled to take hold of the hope offered to us may be greatly encouraged. We have this hope as an anchor for the soul, firm and secure (Heb. 6:17–19).

In other words, when we look ahead, we have hope because the God we trust is trustworthy.

Something of the same note is struck by the Hebrew word *yahal.* But this word tends to focus more on our present experience than on the future. An emphasis on the present is seen in some translations of this Hebrew term as "wait." If we look at passages in which this word appears, we find a distinctive emphasis. We wait in hope because God is by nature the deliverer of his people. We know God will act to save us as we hope in him. We wait in hope because it is fitting, when God brings us endless days of inactivity, to wait, confident, until God does act.

In each of these two Hebrew terms is the certainty that we who know God can trust him. And that certainty infuses our Old Testament with confidence. Because the psalmist knows and trusts God, he can say, "I will always have hope" (Ps. 71:14). With hope, you and I find the courage we need to meet each new day. We know that "the Lord preserves the faithful. . . . Be strong and take heart, all you who hope in the Lord" (Ps. 31:23–24).

The great contribution that our Old Testament makes to our understanding of hope is this: *Hope* is a relational term. It is an affirmation of trust in God. We hope, not because we know what is ahead, but because we know that God is trustworthy. "You have given me hope," David writes in Psalm 119:49–50. "My comfort in my suffering is this: your promise renews my life." So the Old Testament exhorts you and me to have hope by trusting God. "Put your hope in the Lord, for with the Lord is unfailing love, and with him is full redemption" (Ps. 130:7).

> Find rest, O my soul, in God alone.
> My hope comes from him.
> He alone is my rock and my salvation;
>   he is my fortress, I will not be shaken (Ps. 62:5–6).

The Greek word for hope, *elpis*, is found most often in the New Testament epistles. There it is invariably used to signify the expectation of something good. As in the Old Testament, hope is seen in the New Testament as something we must wait for. The object of our hope is not something we possess now. But the New Testament differs from the Old in that it tends to spell out more clearly the good things that God, the one in whom we hope, has in mind for us.

What are some of the things for which believers can hope?

For one thing, there is resurrection. Because all believers will be raised to be with the Lord, the sorrow of separation from loved ones takes on a new aspect. We grieve, but not as "the rest of men who have no hope" (1 Thess. 4:13).

Looking beyond history to eternity, we see many other blessings associated with resurrection. Jesus will appear, and we will be with him (see Titus 2:13; 1 John 3:2–3). Our bodies, subject now to aging and illness, will be liberated with the whole creation from bondage to decay (Rom. 8:20, 24). At that time we will experience fully all that it means to have eternal life; at that time we will enter into the inheritance God has reserved for us (Titus 1:2, 3:7; 1 Pet. 1:3).

The New Testament also talks about hope for things that will happen in this life. One thing that it emphasizes is transformation—a growing renewal of our potential as redeemed human beings. Scripture portrays the Holy Spirit as active in our lives now, inscribing God's holiness on our personalities. We "are being transformed into his likeness with ever-increasing glory, which comes from the Lord, who is the Spirit" (2 Cor. 3:18).

This strong emphasis on our present hope for personal growth is found often in the New Testament. Because of the Holy Spirit's present activity, there is a "righteousness for which we hope" (Gal. 5:5). Christ in us becomes not just the promise of a glorious distant future, but also the promise of a meaningful tomorrow (Col. 1:27; Eph. 1:18–23).

When Eileen talked with Sue on the phone, and when she met with Sue and others in her small Tuesday group, it was clear that discouragement was taking a terrible toll. Her eyes were dull and lifeless. She spoke in a tiny, fearful voice. Her hair was unwashed, her clothing unkempt.

Eileen told the group how hard it was to get up mornings. How hard it was even to decide to do her wash. She couldn't face going outside to shop, and the idea of looking for a job or getting more education was unbearable. Eileen, without hope, could not even cope with life's commonplace activities, much less take the responsible daily steps which would lead her into a different future.

The New Testament recognizes times like these and speaks of the powerful subjective impact of hope on our times of discouragement. When we look beyond today and hope for the good God has in store for us, we taste the wonders of God's transformation. The certainty that God has good in store for us moves us to an energizing "faith and love" which "spring from" hope (Col. 1:5; see 1 John 3:3; Titus 1:2).

The New Testament also associates hope with character. Character is developed as we endure our times of waiting, "inspired by hope in our Lord Jesus Christ" (1 Thess. 1:3; Rom. 5:4–5). We are encouraged in Scripture to "hold on to our courage and the hope of which we boast" (Heb. 3:6) and to make our hope sure by showing "diligence to the very end" (Heb. 6:11).

Hope, then, gives us the courage to keep on when life turns dark. Hope is the source of an inner strength which exists despite our circumstances.

But there is more. Hope also bring us a sense of joy (Rom. 12:12). With hope we can maintain an optimistic outlook on life, even when we are trapped in waiting (1 Pet. 3:15; 1 Thess. 1:3). Life will continue to hold its stress, and waiting will continue to hurt. But the believer whose hope is in the Lord, who has a grasp of God's determination to do us good, will not be overcome.

As we struggle to understand God's timing in our lives, we cannot overlook hope.

Hope is something that you and I can experience only in times of pain, as we wait for some relief. If God did not make us wait, we would never know the comfort of a sharper focus on our relationship with God. We would never

know the reevaluation of priorities that comes with awareness of eternity. We would never know the significance that
God places on what happens *within* us as well as what
happens *to* us. And we would never discover the fact
that hope in God provides strength, enabling us to go on
when the last strength we have is swallowed up in discouragement.

God has a reason for all he does.

He has a reason for his timing.

And one reason for God's timing is to give us hope.

How wonderful, then, to remember and to hold "unswerv-
ingly to the hope we profess," knowing that "he who promised is faithful" (Heb. 10:23). How good to find in God's
word clear statements of his fixed intention to bless. "For
I know the plans I have for you," declares the Lord, "plans
to prosper you and not to harm you, plans to give you
hope and a future" (Jer. 29:11).

Encouraged by Sue and the others in her small group,
Eileen, a Christian, is experiencing a rebirth of hope. At
their last meeting, her hair was washed and curled, her
clothing attractive. She's still hesitant, but now she talks
of little things that show she has begun to take charge of
her life.

The tragedy of her divorce, the apparent meaninglessness
of her time of waiting, have permitted Eileen to discover
the power of hope.

What does the Bible's teaching on hope say to you and
me as we wait on God's timing?

(1) *Hope is a powerful resource God offers to every believer.*
Hope is for each of us because hope does not depend on
what we do or do not do. If you or I had hope only because
of our intelligence, or our good looks, or our money, or
our faithfulness to God, some of us would be stripped of
hopefulness. We're not all intelligent, or handsome, or

wealthy. And we all fall short in our relationship with God. But the Christian's hope is not based on human qualities. It is rooted securely in the character of God.

God is always faithful to his commitments. And God is fully committed to you and to me in Jesus Christ. It is because we know who God is and what he is like that we have hope.

(2) *Hope can only be experienced during those times when God says, "Wait."* We never hope for something we already possess. So hope is always generated by a sense of lack. I could never say, "I hope for two cars," because we do have two cars. I could never say, "I have hope for children"; our house is full of them. No, it's only when we sense a lack, when there is a gap in our lives that must be filled, that hope comes into play.

It may well be that God gives us times of waiting, times of need, times when we yearn for release, just so we can have the benefits of hope.

Hope anchors our soul in the character of God.

Hope gives us strength when ours is spent.

Hope stimulates our inner transformation.

While it is not easy for us to think of the pain of waiting in terms of blessing, it may be that only through hope can some of God's richest blessings become ours.

(3) *Hope has an impact on our present experience.* Through God's gift of hope, of the confident expectation that his future is good, we find the strength to keep on. We find the courage to cope.

This is a wonderful thing about God.

He may ask us to wait. He may give us months and years that are empty of things we deeply desire. But he never leaves us alone.

He gives us his own presence.

As we hope in him, he gives us the strength to go on.

And, as a beacon calling us to his bright future, his promise remains, unshakeable and firm: "'I know the plans I have for you,' declares the Lord, 'plans to prosper you and not to harm you, plans to give you hope and a future'" (Jer. 29:11).

For Meditation or Discussion

1. Which verse on "hope" quoted in this chapter is most meaningful to you? Using a concordance, look for other verses on hope which encourage or strengthen you.

2. If you were to imagine your situation ten years from now, what is the "best" future you could envision? Take time to describe that future carefully and in detail, trying to envision everything about it that is important to you.

3. Think carefully about the kind of person you want to become. What qualities of character are important to you? How do you suppose "hope" may be used by God to help you become this kind of person?

9

Hear My Cry

I met Lil this past Tuesday evening at a meeting where I spoke on "hope." She was in the second row—a tall blonde woman of about fifty with a rugged but attractive face. Throughout my talk, Lil kept interrupting, her remarks showing how bitterly she felt her own despair and hopelessness.

After I finished, Lil came over to speak to me personally. She shared how much she hated this compulsion she felt to speak up about herself. "I'm terrified," Lil confessed. "I don't know what's happening to me."

Lil was catapulted into her own agonizing waiting time by the death of her parents. Shortly afterward, she sold the family home, which had been theirs for over a hundred years. She went to Florida for four months, gradually losing her zest for life and her sense of direction. Returning to Michigan, Lil moved from her small town to a larger city. She found a room with a friendly woman and kept busy on her job, but plummeted deeper into despair.

What frightens Lil most is that she no longer knows herself. She has always been a friendly, active person. "When anyone was hurting, they always came to me," Lil told me. "I was the one who took people meals, held the hands of the dying, and cheered up the discouraged. I don't know myself any more, and I'm scared."

Lil is afraid to move into an apartment by herself. She's afraid she'll just sit there staring at the walls—even though she continues to be so active she's seldom home. Lil is afraid she'll never pull out of her depression, never recover her optimistic outlook on life. She is terrified that she'll keep on saying and doing things she hates, frightened that her loss of self-control may mean she's heading toward a mental institution.

Lil is sure that life can hold no meaning for her, but is unwilling and afraid to die. And Lil no longer knows how to pray.

Waiting can rob any of us of the comfort of prayer, particularly if we misunderstand prayer's nature. Prayer, especially while we are waiting on God's timing, is far more than just telling God what we want or need.

Making requests is, of course, an important aspect of prayer. When Sue lost Pat to his dad, she found herself often begging the Lord to let her son come back. And she was able to find significant comfort in this prayer. "Do not be anxious about anything," the Bible says, "but in everything, by prayer and petition, with thanksgiving, present your requests to God. And the peace of God, which transcends all understanding, will guard your hearts and your minds in Christ Jesus" (Phil. 4:6–7).

Even before her request was answered and Pat did come home, Sue discovered that just the process of asking, of putting her needs in God's hands, brought a sense of peace. That peace would be swept away at times by fresh anxiety. But Sue could always pray again, and as she prayed she found that the Holy Spirit actively guarded her heart and mind.

So prayer as petition always has a part in our lives, even in our times of waiting.

But what if we, like Lil, reach the point in our waiting

that we don't even know what to ask for—or how to pray? What about times when we, like Lil, hurt so much that there is nothing specific we want, nothing we can think of that seems likely to give our life meaning?

It can be helpful, during such times, to expand our concept of prayer beyond "request and petition." We need to understand prayer simply as communication, as talking with God.

Three things about prayer as communication seem particularly important for those who wait:

(1) *Prayer flows from and expresses relationship*. The disciples couldn't help noticing. Jesus, despite the press of the crowds and the draining days he spent teaching and healing, often slipped away alone for prayer. One day, when Jesus finished praying and rejoined his followers, the disciples asked him, "Lord, teach us to pray" (Luke 11:1). Jesus proceeded to give them a basic prayer, a pattern, which has particular meaning for us who wait. It is particularly significant because it expresses clearly the nature of the relationship with God that sustains us. This prayer, which is commonly called the Lord's Prayer, is familiar to us all:

> Father,
>   hallowed be your name,
> your kingdom come.
> Give us each day our daily bread.
> Forgive us our sins,
>   for we also forgive everyone who sins against us,
> And lead us not into temptation (Luke 11:2–4).

"Father." When it hurts too much to wait and we don't know how to pray, this is how to begin. Come to God and cry, "Father."

This first word captures the nature of our relationship

with God and expresses our sense of need. We remember that in Jesus we are God's dearly loved children. We cry out, overwhelmed, rushing like dependent children to daddy to be comforted, to have everything made all right.

God is a Father, and like a loving father, he does care for his children. We may not know what to pray for or how to ask, but in our pain we can cry out again and again, "Father!"

"Hallowed be your name." Our relationship with God is an intimate family relationship, rich in warmth and comfort and security. It is made secure by the fact that the one who is our Father is truly God. Jesus' prayer invites us to remember who our Father is, holding him in full respect. *Father* is not an empty word, nor are our hopes empty, when the one we count on is Almighty God, the Sovereign Lord of the universe.

"Your kingdom come." The kingdom of God is not just his overarching rule of the universe, nor is it just that era of history to come when Jesus will rule on earth. The kingdom of God is present wherever and whenever his people fully acknowledge him, submit to his will, and expect him to act. The kingdom is created by our acknowledging and submitting to God and expecting him to work.

In our waiting times, "your kingdom come" is a prayer which expresses our willingness to do God's will and our confidence that God can work his good in our world of space and time.

In a significant way, this prayer is an expression of surrender. We release ourselves and our situation to the Lord, placing everything in his hands. "Your kingdom come" says that we are willing to let the God who is our Father exercise his sovereign control in our lives. You and I find peace in the surrender of this release.

"Give us each day our daily bread." Life can only be

lived one day at a time. We cannot know what our tomorrows will bring. Prayer for daily bread keeps us sensitive to the fact that we remain daily dependent on God. Such dependence is not unhealthy, but promises us release from fear of the future. Whatever tomorrow may hold for us, God's larder is full. He will provide us with our daily bread. He will meet each need when that need occurs.

"Forgive us our sins." When discouraged and waiting, we're apt to focus on the darker side of life. Lil is stunned at the way she behaves these days, ashamed of her domineering actions and her constant intrusions on others. How important to remember that God's love is not withdrawn when we fail! We may be overwhelmed by our sins and failures, but this prayer reminds us that God knows how to deal with sins. He forgives. And the deep love he feels for us remains unshaken.

God sets a pattern in his forgiveness that can release us from another great problem. How do we respond to those who hurt us? Dwelling on real or imagined sins in others can drive us to discouragement or bitterness. But God teaches us by his example that you and I need not withdraw. We, too, can forgive.

"Lead us not into temptation." Confident in God's continuing love, we can freely ask the Lord not to place us in situations that hold more pressure than we can survive. This final request is again an act of commitment. We commit our tomorrows into God's hands, acknowledging his right to lead us, asking only that any trials not be transformed into temptations.

For Lil, then, and for you and me when we simply do not know how to pray, Jesus' prayer provides us with a pattern, a model. Lil is hurting now, fearful and uncertain and close to despair. She does not even feel capable of asking for help. But Lil can cry out, "Father." In the simplest of words, Lil can express her relationship to a God whose will is best and whose tomorrows hold not the terrors she fears, but God's supply of her every need.

(2) *Prayer involves a free expression of emotions to God.* Prayer, as taught in Jesus' model prayer, flows from and expresses our relationship with the Lord. But prayer also involves a free expression of our emotions to God.

Lil is ashamed to find herself talking about her feelings and her despair with everyone she meets. But Lil need never fear that she is imposing on God.

The Bible's prayer book, the Psalms, shows how freely the believer is to express *every* feeling to the Lord. This includes not only positive feelings such as joy and thankfulness, but also negative feelings such as anger and bitterness.

A sampling of the Psalms reveals the range of negative feelings and actual complaints that godly persons have expressed to God. As we read them today, we sense the cry of hurting hearts—hearts that ache as much as Lil's, as much as yours and mine:

> How long, O Lord? Will you forget me forever?
>   How long will you hide your face from me?
> How long must I wrestle with my thoughts
>   and every day have sorrow in my heart? (Ps. 13:1–2).

> Be merciful to me, O Lord, for I am in distress;
>   my eyes grow weak with sorrow,
>   my soul and my body with grief.
> My life is consumed by anguish
>   and my years by groaning;
> my strength fails because of my affliction,
>   and my bones grow weak (Ps. 31:9–10).

> My heart is in anguish within me;
>   the terrors of death assail me.

Fear and trembling have beset me;
    horror has overwhelmed me.
I said, "Oh, that I had the wings of a dove!
    I would fly away and be at rest—
I would flee far away
    and stay in the desert;
I would hurry to my place of shelter,
    far from the tempest and storm!" (Ps.55: 4–8).

My soul is full of trouble
    and my life draws near the grave.
I am counted among those who go down to the pit;
    I am like a man without strength.
I am set apart with the dead,
    like the slain who lie in the grave,
whom you remember no more,
    who are cut off from your care.
You have put me in the lowest pit,
    in the darkest depths.
Your wrath lies heavily upon me;
    you have overwhelmed me with all your waves.
You have taken from me my closest friends
    and have made me repulsive to them.
I am confined and cannot escape;
    my eyes are dim with grief.
I call to you, O Lord, every day;
    I spread out my hands to you.
Do you show your wonders to the dead?
    Do those who are dead rise up and praise you? . . .
But I cry to you for help, O Lord;
    in the morning my prayer comes before you.
Why, O Lord, do you reject me
    and hide your face from me? (Ps. 88:3–10, 13–14).

. . . my days vanish like smoke;
    my bones burn like glowing embers.
My heart is blighted and withered like grass;
    I forget to eat my food.

Because of my loud groaning
    I am reduced to skin and bones.
I am like a desert owl,
    like an owl among the ruins.
I lie awake; I have become
    like a bird alone on a housetop.
All day long my enemies taunt me;
    those who rail against me use my name as a curse.
For I eat ashes as my food
    and mingle my drink with tears
because of your great wrath,
    for you have taken me up and thrown me aside
(Ps. 102:3–10).

These and other psalms help us identify our own emotions when they emerge under the stress of waiting. They also help us realize that we are free to share our deepest selves with the Lord.

One of Lil's greatest problems is that when she tries to share her feelings with others, her very intensity drives others away from her. The church she goes to has a singles' group—some fifty people of different ages. The relationships developed in the group are not deep, and the meetings tend to feature a superficial, "fun" atmosphere. After breaking in on fun activities with expressions of her own pain, Lil was told that the meetings were obviously causing her pain because she wasn't ready to have fun—and the group stopped sending her notification of their activities!

Perhaps we can understand. It's not just that people don't like to listen to other's troubles. Troubles make most of us uncomfortable. Someone hurts, and we don't know what to do or say. Or we have troubles of our own and don't feel capable of taking on others'. And so most of us simply turn away—sympathetic perhaps, but unwilling to be involved.

God isn't like that.

He won't offer us a quick solution, but he will listen.

And God will care. Our despair won't drive him away from us. He'll sit down, draw close to us, and never remove his gaze as we talk about our hurts and fears.

And it's important for us to talk.

We need to acknowledge our emotions, to identify and express them. We need to share them, especially with God, because part of the healing process is airing our wounds.

Prayer, when we don't know how to pray because it hurts too much to wait, should involve expression of our emotions to the Lord. And, just in case we can't put our feelings into words, God has given us psalms like those I've quoted, so we can pray along with the psalmists.

If you hurt, and you don't know what to say to God, and one of the psalms you've read strikes a chord in your heart, make that psalm your prayer and pour out your feelings to the Lord.

(3) *Prayer also, as part of our total relationship with the Lord, involves us in remembrance and praise.*

It's striking. In each of the pain-filled psalms I've quoted except for the 88th, the expression of feelings moves us beyond despair. In talking with God, we shift our focus from ourselves to him. And we remember his goodness, his faithfulness, his care.

In Psalm 13, David, after expressing the pain of his waiting, says,

> But I trust in your unfailing love;
>   my heart rejoices in your salvation.
> I will sing to the Lord,
>   for he has been good to me (vv. 13:5–6).

In Psalm 31, David again affirms his trust, and is moved to praise:

But I trust in you, O Lord;
 I say, "You are my God."
My times are in your hands (vv. 14–15).

Praise be to the Lord,
 for he showed his wonderful love to me. . . .
Love the Lord, all his saints!
 The Lord preserves the faithful,
 but the proud he pays back in full.
Be strong and take heart,
 all you who hope in the Lord (vv. 21–24).

In Psalm 102, contemplation of the Lord leads the psalmist, "an afflicted man" who writes "when he is faint and pours out his lament before the Lord," to remembrance and to praise:

In the beginning you laid the foundations of the earth,
 and the heavens are the work of your hands.
They will perish, but you remain;
 they will all wear out like a garment.
Like clothing you will change them
 and they will be discarded.
But you remain the same,
 and your years will never end.
The children of your servants will live in your presence;
 their descendants will be established before you (vv. 25–28).

When you and I are afflicted and faint, we are invited to pour out our laments to the Lord. Gradually, as we do, the Holy Spirit will shift the focus of our awareness. He will lead us to remember the nature of the one to whom we speak. Remembering the Lord, our perspective will gradually change.

The surging emotions will begin to still. The fears will quiet; the turbulence will give way to peace. As we remember who God is, our prayer will express trust, and we, too, will find ourselves moved to praise.

What, then, are we to do when waiting hurts so much we don't know how to pray? We can let Scripture itself guide us and, when too choked to find our own words, we can pray along with the Bible's recorded prayers.

- We can follow Jesus' model prayer, given his disciples, and find rest in our relationship with God the Father.
- We can follow the models provided in the Psalms and pour out our emotions to God, sure that he won't be shocked and that he will never reject us.
- And we can follow the patterns of praise also found in the Psalms. As we remember God's faithfulness and all the good he has done for his people, and as we begin to praise, we'll discover that prayer brings peace even to people who wait.

For Meditation or Discussion

1. What place has prayer had in your personal experience? How have you found your prayer life affected in your own times of waiting?

2. Which of the Bible passages quoted in this chapter best expresses what you feel and where you are right now? Can you find several other verses in Psalms that express your present emotional state and attitude?

3. When you think of prayer as total communication with God, in which area do you feel you most need to grow? In making requests, affirming relationship, expressing feelings, offering praise? Or in another area?

10

In the Last Time

The Bible's great hall of fame honoring those who lived by faith contains two poignant, brief passages. The first reads:

> All these people were still living by faith when they died. They did not receive the things promised; they only saw them and welcomed them from a distance. . . . They were longing for a better country—a heavenly one. Therefore God is not ashamed to be called their God, for he has prepared a city for them (Heb. 11:13–16).

They waited all their lives.

And still they did not receive what God had promised.

So far in our exploration of God's timing, we've looked ahead with great optimism. We may wait now. But the time of waiting will pass, and we'll receive the good that God has in mind for us. I've insisted, with the psalmists, that as we wait on the Lord it is with the confident expectation that God will act.

But it doesn't always happen that way—at least not in this life.

Last November my dad began to have trouble eating. Things didn't taste good. Eating made his stomach hurt.

The problem gradually got worse until in early spring my sister and I insisted he see his doctor.

The results of the first tests were ambiguous. The doctor who has treated the family for decades was encouraging and prescribed various pills. But the pains grew worse.

Finally, we insisted on tests administered by the specialist who'd treated our stepmother the year before. My sister and I went together to hear the report; Dad didn't feel up to it.

We heard what we expected to hear: "Your dad's full of cancer. It's in his back, in his bones, in his chest and stomach. I don't recommend treatment. He has maybe six weeks or a couple of months."

I moved in with Dad to live those last weeks with him. We didn't talk much; he didn't feel well enough. But I remember one afternoon especially.

Dad was sitting in his favorite chair, hunched forward.

"It doesn't seem right," he said. "All my life I've fought things. Now I can't fight. All I can do is wait. It doesn't seem right."

Sometimes all we can do is wait.

And wait without hope.

My Aunt Genie is another person who waits, knowing that for her there will be no wonderful change as God's timing brings her relief.

Aunt Genie spent most of her life as a schoolteacher, working with first and second graders in Ecorse, Michigan. For the last fifteen years, she has been confined to her apartment in Ann Arbor. Aunt Genie has crippling arthritis. Her hands are warped and twisted, her muscles ache, and only an electrically operated chair that lifts her in and out enables her to sit down.

Aunt Genie waits, affected now with an eye problem that has made it impossible for her even to read or watch TV.

Aunt Genie waits, and nothing suggests that God's timing will reverse the ravages of her disease or release her from her rooms.

It's true that both my dad, who died at eighty-six, and my Aunt Genie, who is in her late seventies, have lived a long and full life. In the normal course, you and I, too, must near the end of our time on earth. Waiting then may well be waiting for a unique release found in death.

But age isn't a full answer for questions raised about those who wait without ever experiencing the release that God's timing seems to promise.

Years ago, Sue was in Germany with her first husband, who was in the army at the time. They lived "on the economy," renting a German apartment away from military housing. And Sue was pregnant with their first child.

Pregnancy is a special kind of waiting. You can feel the child grow, pushing out your belly. Then, as the infant quickens, you can feel movement inside. You shift your body when you lie down, trying to find a comfortable position as you feel the weight of the new life growing inside. You wait eagerly for the next sturdy kick that reassures you and tells you that your waiting time will pass.

While Sue waited, she decorated one room in the little apartment. There was a baby bed, a changing table, a dresser and mirror, and of course those little touches that every mother adds as she waits—a stuffed animal, a panel of childish wallpaper, a touch of pink and blue paint.

Sue knew how long her wait would be. And she knew the good that God would bring her when the wait was over—a child to love and care for, a child who would occupy her time during the long days and nights when her husband was on duty.

She knew how long her wait would be.

But she was wrong.

When the time came, Sue was rushed to the military hospital. For over a day, she was in labor—labor that drained her of her strength. Finally, the baby began to come—breech. In a stunning display of incompetence, the medical team made mistake after mistake. Finally, an exhausted Sue heard the doctor say, "she's out." The words released Sue from her unbearable effort, and she relaxed.

But the baby wasn't out.

Sue relaxed, and her cervix closed, trapping the baby's head inside her body.

By the time the doctors got the baby out, Sue was nearly dead from loss of blood. And Jennifer, Sue's first child, was gone.

The long wait of pregnancy was over.

But tragedy, not release, was at its end.

Later one of the doctors, a doctor not on the team present at the delivery, told Sue, "I was just about to do a Caesarean on you. But I saw I was supposed to go off duty." Over a day in labor. A breech delivery. With perhaps only ten minutes difference in timing, a different doctor would have operated and little Jennifer would have lived.

God's timing doesn't promise that everything will always turn out right. We don't always receive the things we're waiting for.

The second passage in Hebrews 11 says it clearly:

Some faced jeers and flogging, while still others were chained and put in prison. They were stoned; they were sawed in two; they were put to death by the sword. They went about in sheepskins and goatskins, destitute, persecuted and mistreated —the world was not worthy of them. They wandered in deserts and mountains, and in caves and holes in the ground.

These were all commended for their faith, yet none of them received what had been promised (vv. 36–39).

How does this affect our outlook as you and I wait on God's timing? We have no guarantee during our time of waiting that we'll experience the proverbial "happy ending." We, too, may be commended for our faith but never "receive what has been promised."

As I think back over my father's life, I realize how much he had to wait. His body broken by a fall from a dam as a young man, he waited years for healing. Later, a withered esophagus kept him from swallowing. After years of struggle, his sturdy one-hundred-eighty-pound frame wasted to less than one hundred twenty, he went through an operation he wasn't expected to survive. But he did survive.

His health restored a few years later, my dad was driving the car when he and my mother had an accident. My mother died in that accident, and Dad was catapulted into a half-dozen long years of loneliness. Then he met again and married a woman who had lived next door as I grew up. Dad and Frances had eight wonderfully happy years together before she was stricken with cancer.

Dad lived through Frances's illness, hoping against hope that her cancer could be halted. Then Frances died, and Dad wept. Once again he was alone.

I had moved closer to him by then. Dad and I were able to go fishing together, and I was able to visit him at least once a week.

But then came the cancer.

In just a few weeks, Dad was gone.

Dad's life, like each of our lives, had been a tapestry woven with strands of tragedy and blessing, with times of agonizing, empty waiting and times of hopes fulfilled.

As Dad and I waited together in the house where I grew up, we talked. "I'd hoped for just one more summer of fishing," he said once. But mostly we talked about his future. About the two wonderful women whom he'd loved, and who were waiting for him.

"Won't they be excited! You'll have more hugs and kisses than you can stand."

That's right.

We Christians share the conviction that the meaning of human existence isn't found in this life alone. We believe death for the individual believer isn't the end, but instead is our passage into a full experience of the eternal life God has given us in Jesus. Because our life is endless and eternity bright, we share the Apostle Paul's conviction that "our present sufferings are not worth comparing with the glory that will be revealed in us" (Rom. 8:18).

When we think of waiting and of God's timing, we need to remember that God's plan may involve blessing and release that comes not *during* this life, but *after* this life is over.

Some have criticized Christianity as promising nothing but "pie in the sky bye and bye." As we've already seen in our exploration of God's timing, Christianity does no such thing. Trust in God and in his timing gives us strength for today and hope for tomorrow. We know that God is at work—now. We wait on God, confident that he intends to do us good, and so with Christ in our life we have "hope and a future."

But there are still cases in which God's timing calls for us to wait out the months or years of our lifetime and find release only after death. Paul, in his affirmation of resurrection, argues strongly that "if only for this life we have hope in Christ, we are to be pitied more than all men" (1 Cor. 15:19). You and I can truly understand the glorious good God has for us only when we evaluate our present experience in view of the blessings and eternal rewards that await us.

The promise of resurrection beyond this present life is found in both Old and New Testaments, although it is affirmed most powerfully in the New. Job, despite his tragic losses and his suffering, cried,

> I know that my Redeemer lives,
>   and that in the end he will stand upon the earth.
> And after my skin has been destroyed,
>   yet in my flesh I will see God.
> I myself will see him!
>   with my own eyes—I, and not another.
> How my heart yearns within me (Job 19:25–27).

And so we do look forward, beyond time, to an eternity in which all things are made right and all mysteries solved. In his great mercy God has

> given us new birth into a living hope through the resurrection of Jesus Christ from the dead, and into an inheritance that can never perish, spoil or fade—kept in heaven for you who through faith are shielded by God's power until the coming of the salvation that is ready to be revealed in the last time (1 Pet. 1:3–5).

Not only is an inheritance reserved for us, but we ourselves are shielded by God's power, guarded until the time full salvation comes.

What does the Christian perspective on eternity add to our understanding of God's timing?

(1) *The good which God promises is doubly assured.* Like my father's, your life and mine will be filled with a mixture of joys and sorrow. Neither total tragedy nor total happiness will be our lot. For most of us, the times of waiting will pass and God will bring us a present release, capping our time of trial with his own rich blessings.

But when the times of waiting stretch out endlessly or when life nears an end and there is no relief in sight, we need to remember that God's promise to do good to his people is an eternal commitment. Our tragedies—and our times of waiting—cannot be evaluated in terms of this life alone.

This past Mother's Day Sue and two of her friends, Yvette and Yvonne, shared lunch. They talked about children and gifts, and Sue shared that she had gotten herself three presents—one for each of her children.

"Three?"

"Yes, three. One for Pat and Sarah. And one for Jennifer."

There were tears in Yvonne's eyes. Married some fifteen years, she has no children, but has had three miscarriages.

"You know, Vonnie," Sue said, resting her hand lightly on her friend's arm, "you can get yourself three presents too. Your children are there now, waiting for you."

Yvonne may never on earth know an end to her long, painful wait for a family. But when death is swallowed up in fresh new life, the family Yvonne yearns for will be gloriously hers.

God is guarding her inheritance.

And God is shielding her, through faith, to receive one day all that he has promised.

(2) *Hope is not for this life only.* I remember once visiting my dad during his lonely years of waiting after mom died. I flew in to Grand Rapids, Michigan, for a meeting. Dad met me afterward, and we headed north in his camper, hauling his Boston Whaler. I fished and played cards with him for two days, and then he brought me back to the airport.

It was raining, a dreary spring day. He slumped in the seat beside me, his pipe clutched in his teeth, trying not to look depressed and alone. I got my suitcase, shook his hand, and tried to smile as I said goodbye. But my heart was breaking for him.

The day of his funeral was different. It was another spring day. The sun was shining and the wind blustery. His lodge brothers conducted their graveside service, following the funeral service which I had preached, and Dad's ashes were laid to rest beside the remains of my mother.

And though I missed him, my heart was glad.

Dad was no longer depressed, no longer alone, but surrounded by his loved ones and in the presence of the Lord.

How good to know that one day, in God's "last time," all our waiting will be over, and all our pain swallowed up in joy!

(3) *God's timing remains in his own hands.* What does the future hold for you and me? Is it to be a brief wait, such as the three years of anguish that Sue knew before God acted to restore her family and provide a new love? Or is it to be a lifelong wait, such as the painful years Aunt Genie endures, with no prospect of improvement?

We cannot know. But what we *can* know is that God's timing will ultimately bring us to joy. No absolute guarantee of joy in this life is to be found in Christian faith. But there is the guarantee of strength and hope for today, of a present that is important, and of a rich inheritance beyond.

Some time ago I read a story that has remained in my mind. It was the story of a missionary who returned to the United States after years abroad. As his plane landed, he found the airport filled with eager crowds gathered to welcome some political figure home from a trip abroad. Bands played and people cheered.

But there was no one there to meet the missionary— not even a representative of his mission. Wearily he carried his bags to a taxi and gave the address of a cheap hotel. That night, heartsick and alone, he sat in his room. He was filled with self-pity. There had been no crowds for him. No one had cheered when he came home. No one had even noticed his arrival.

And then, suddenly, it struck him.

"I'm not home yet!"

And then he could visualize it—the bands playing, the crowds cheering, all the loved ones gathering around him with the hundreds won during his years of service. All his. When he reached home.

That's what's ahead for you and me in God's last time. When we come home—to heaven, to loved ones, and to him.

For Meditation or Discussion

1. Imagine your own homecoming to heaven. What about it will bring you the greatest joy?

2. Read Hebrews 11 several times. How did God's timing reveal itself in the lives of those chronicled there? How often was waiting a necessary element in their triumphs of faith?

3. Why do you suppose Paul wrote in 1 Corinthians 15:19 that "if only for this life we have hope in Christ, we are to be pitied more than all men"? What seems to you to be the most significant thing about resurrection that the Bible teaches in this key New Testament passage?

11

Faith and Patience

Jennifer would have been ten years old today. Sue lay in bed, quiet tears wetting her cheeks. She folded her arms across her chest, and suddenly it all flooded back. She knew she had lain just that way ten years ago, the day Jennifer had died, the day Sue had almost died with her in childbirth.

Suddenly Sue was reliving the experience. She felt herself outside her body, clutching the personality of her first child to her heart. She heard the voices that told her to let go, that she must stay until the time came for her to join Jennifer. Overwhelmed anew by the loss of her first child, Sue sobbed.

"Why? Why did I have to wait? Why couldn't I go with Jennifer? I shouldn't have let her go!"

There are times for all of us when waiting is unbearable. Not because we are so eager for what's ahead, perhaps, but because we feel so empty and deprived now. What are we to do when waiting brings to you and me that sense of unbearable loss and emptiness? How are we to deal with an unbearable present?

Lil, who lost her hopeful outlook when a series of tragedies struck, knows that unbearably empty feeling. Pam has known it. You and I have experienced it, too. Waiting can color our outlook, shading everything such a dull grey that nothing seems meaningful any more.

Those feelings may last for a moment, as they did with Sue on the tenth anniversary of Jennifer's birth, or they may cast their pall over us for weeks and months on end. But when these feelings do come, God has a word for us: Have faith, and have patience.

Faith and patience are linked together in two passages of Scripture designed to give us perspective when life seems meaningless. In Hebrews 6, the writer reminds his readers of God's fairness. Nothing we do from love, to help God's people, will go unrewarded, he says. "We want each of you to show this same diligence to the very end. . . . We do not want you to become lazy, but to imitate those who through faith and patience inherit what has been promised" (vv. 11–12).

God's promise lies ahead, reassuring us that life does have a goal. But while we wait, we are to show diligence. Faith, linked with patience, encourages us to make today count and reminds us that how we live each day does have meaning.

The other passage reinforces this message with an image from farming: "Be patient, then, brothers, until the Lord's coming," writes James. "See how the farmer waits for the land to yield its valuable crop and how patient he is for the fall and spring rains. You too, be patient and stand firm, because the Lord's coming is near" (James 5:7–8).

Valuable crops don't appear overnight. Valuable crops must grow, and growth involves waiting.

I understand a little about farming. I was twelve when I began to understand. Dad slipped the reins around my shoulder, and I gripped the wooden handles of the plow. "Gidup," I said to the old grey horse that stood there, tail swishing rhythmically.

During that summer on my grandfather's farm, I plowed,

harrowed, planted, and cultivated, using horses because gas was still rationed in 1943. I felt the earth turn as I struggled to follow the plow. I watched the clay broken and smoothed under the iron teeth of the drag. (The soil had to be broken if healthy crops were to grow.)

That summer I watched the seeds I had planted sprout. I sweated in the sun and bent over a hoe. And later, when the plants were higher, I rode a two-horse cultivator between the rows.

I was only twelve, but I remember how long the summer seemed, and how slowly the plants grew. It seemed forever until the corn I planted began to ripen; it was forever and a day until harvest time arrived.

Farming is like that, because growth is like that. Growth is a process, a slow and measured unfolding. The promise of what the mature plant will be is buried deep within the seed. But the fulfillment of that promise—the harvest of a valuable crop—comes only after growth's long wait.

This is why our waiting times are really full of promise, even though life may seem empty and meaningless.

You and I have been called to wait because we are growing things, too. God has buried within us his own vision of what we are to become. Our times of waiting hurt, but growing times were never intended to be times of fulfillment.

This is why both faith and patience are important. Faith reminds us that God is faithful and that fulfillment does lie ahead. Patience enables us to make the most of the time God has given us for growth.

The waiting times may feel empty and grey, but they are never meaningless. The ground must be broken. The storms must come. Young plants must send their roots deep, drawing strength from every experience, growing strong and healthy. In time, the promised inheritance will come.

The Bible also teaches us how to wait productively. We find a hint in the Greek word that our English versions translate as "patience." That Greek word emphasizes self-control. It expresses an ability to keep on despite circumstances that could distract us or agitate our emotions. Patience involves an inner restraint that lets us keep on grow ing even though life may seem empty and our days seem meaningless.

The New Testament, linking the images of growth and productivity, tells us to apply the patience that God provides. A beautiful passage in Colossians 1, a prayer of the Apostle Paul, helps us sense what should be the focus of our efforts as we wait. Paul says that he constantly asks God to

> fill you with the knowledge of his will through all spiritual wisdom and understanding. And we pray this in order that you may live a life worthy of the Lord and may please him in every way: bearing fruit in every good work, growing in the knowledge of God, being strengthened with all power according to his glorious might so that you may have great endurance and patience, and joyfully giving thanks to the Father, who has qualified you to share in the inheritance of the saints in the kingdom light (vv. 9–12).

When we understand this prayer, we catch a vision of how to make our own empty times, when waiting seems to rob us of meaning, times of productive growth.

"Filled with a knowledge of his will." The idea of "God's will" is complex. We think of "God's will for our life," and for many this suggests a specific plan, a pathway marked out for each individual that he or she is to find and follow. Others may think of "God's will" as what the Lord specifically directs and controls in history. Still others think of "God's will" as suffering or troubles that God permits. "It's God's will," they'll say, hoping to assuage the pain.

But in the Colossian prayer, the phrase indicates "that which God has willed" and focuses our attention on God's *revealed* will as found in Scripture. This is where God unveils his thoughts and purpose—and where the cycle of growth for God's people begins.

Scripture is the first place to turn when we are going through a time of waiting. Sometimes we'll read and simply be comforted. But there is more for us in the Bible. Exercising patience, that significant self-control which lets us persevere even when things look bleak, means searching God's word for his perspective. We are to seek to understand God's viewpoint, to let God's word shape our values and our choices.

"Through all spiritual wisdom and understanding." This phrase reminds us that Scripture is not simply to be read for information; we are to apply what we find. "Wisdom" and "understanding" are *sophia* and *sunesin.* Each of these two Greek words focuses our attention not on the possession of knowledge but on the use of knowledge.

Does Hebrews portray helping God's people as an expression of love for the Lord (Heb. 6:10)? Then, despite her depression, Lil can look for opportunities to help a brother or sister in need. She can be sensitive to others despite her own pain.

"Live a life worthy of the Lord . . . please him in every way." The process that Paul is describing moves now toward decisive action. It began with a call to look into Scripture to discover God's perspective on the issues of life. It then reminded us that we are to use what we discover in the Bible to evaluate ourselves and our circumstances. The general truths of the Bible are to be applied specifically to our own situation. Now Paul says we are to act decisively and consistently on what we learn, for our calling is to please God "in every way."

This is often the hardest step when the pain of waiting overcomes us. We lose motivation. We know what we should do, but somehow just do not seem to have the energy or courage to do it. But choosing to act isn't dependent on our feelings. We can take one step now. And then the next. Even when despondent, we can exercise faith and patience, and we can live a life worthy of the Lord.

"Bearing fruit in every good work." The Bible speaks of "fruit" as a supernatural product. Fruit is primarily internal; it is experienced as love, joy, peace, patience, and the other good things listed in Galatians 5:22–23. Fruit is also the impact on others of our good works.

"Bearing fruit" is expressed in the Greek in a passive participle. That's because bearing fruit isn't really something that we do; it's something that God the Holy Spirit does. It's something that happens in us and through us as we act in obedience and apply what we discover in God's Word.

Because you and I can bear the Spirit's fruit even while we wait, even waiting times can be spiritually significant. The impact of our wait on others may only be revealed at harvest time, when Jesus comes again. But the budding of fruit in our own personalities can be experienced now as love and even joy.

"Growing in the knowledge of God." This phrase is an exciting one. Paul's cycle of growth begins with a knowledge of "what God has willed"; it begins with information. But then faith enables us to take this information from God seriously, to search for its relationship to our life, and to act on it. Then God the Holy Spirit works in and through our obedience to produce his own fruit. And through this process, you and I grow in our knowledge *of* God.

It's important to realize that knowledge *of* God is not the same thing as knowledge *about* him. We know about God by listening, reading, hearing. But we come to know *God himself* as obedience deepens our personal relationship with the Lord. It's the difference between information and experience, between reading about driving a car and taking the wheel.

Knowing God in a personal, experiential way is vital for us when we wait. We need to sense the touch of his hand, the comfort of his presence. We need the courage that God supernaturally provides and the unexpected sense of peace that calms us despite turmoil.

Paul's prayer reminds us that we can grow spiritually as fruit-filled Christians, and can know God in a deeper, more personal way, if we concentrate on exploring his Word, applying what we discover, and acting obediently on it. And these are things that we can do even as we must wait! These are things that will fill our lives with meaning even when we feel most empty and alone.

The cycle of growth that Paul describes is something that, with faith and patience, you and I can grasp and experience, whatever our circumstances may be.

And, of course, there's more. We're able to launch ourselves on this cycle of growth because God himself strengthens us with "all power according to his glorious might so that you may have great endurance and patience." And as we experience this work of God in our lives, we discover with amazement that we are "joyfully giving thanks to the Father" despite our pain.

In moments when Sue's sense of loss floods back, she longs to be rejoined with little Jennifer, and she wonders why the wait must be so long. Overwhelmed for months now, Lil struggles against despair. Mixed with her fear of the future is that terrible emptiness that comes when nothing seems worthwhile.

The good news for them, and for you and me, is that life is never meaningless. Even our longest and most painful times of waiting are intended to be times for growth.

What do we learn from Scripture about growing that helps us wait patiently?

(1) *We, too, are growing things.* All growth has direction and purpose. The lifeless things in nature experience change. A river moves silt from one location to another. A storm

drops water from clouds formed hundreds of miles away. A stone rolls down a mountain. All such change is merely rearrangement; there is no transformation of the objects involved.

But living things experience change as growth. A seed falls into the ground. It germinates, roots reach down, and a pale sprout struggles up toward the sun.

Rabbits mate. Within the mother rabbit, cells double and redouble. A tiny mite, pink and hairless, with eyes tightly closed, begins to take form. It draws nourishment from its mother's body, and gradually fur is formed. The mite grows, destined to become an alert and leggy creature like its parents.

Where there is life, there is no mere change; there is growth. The character planted within the original cell unfolds, determining the gradual transformation that will bring the living thing to maturity.

We, too, are living, growing beings. As God's children, he has planted his own nature deep within us (cf. 1 Pet. 1:23). Through the experiences of life we, too, grow, moving toward the destiny God has in mind for you and me. One day that destiny will be fulfilled: "What we will be has not yet been made known. But we know that when he [Jesus] appears, we shall be like him, for we will see him as he is" (1 John 3:2).

In the waiting times of our life God is at work, shaping us and helping us grow toward our destiny of being more like Jesus.

(2) *God controls our seasons.* Just as God has patterned nature to fit the needs of growing plants and animals, so God patterns the experiences of your life and mine. At times our days are bright and sunny, warm with the joys that God so often gives. At other times rain pelts us or storms darken our lives. Both the sun and the rain are necessary for healthy growth.

God always measures carefully the pressures that he lets you and me experience. He promises that he will "not let you be tempted beyond what you can bear" (1 Cor. 10:13). But he *will* let us be tempted. He will let us feel pain, know suffering, taste despair. He will not withhold the losses that break our hearts or the emptiness that drains us of hope. God will give us not what we want, but what we need to help us grow.

(3) *Faith and patience are keys to maximizing our growth.* Waiting times are not to be times of inactivity. Instead, we can concentrate on those things which make for personal and spiritual growth.

Paul's Colossian prayer explains the growth process and gives us an exciting promise. We grow as we seek to understand God's revealed will, see how that will relates to our personal situations and daily experiences, and put God's will into practice through obedience. The promise is that when we follow this process, you and I will bear fruit and will deepen our personal relationship with the Lord.

Faith and patience are important because in the pain of waiting we may lose confidence. Faith grasps the promises of God and trusts that tomorrow will be bright despite the present darkness. Patience exercises a self-control that enables us to persevere despite our emotions. And you and I *can* persevere. Whatever our feelings at the moment, life is always meaningful. Even our darkest seasons are intended to help us grow. And even in our darkest hours, you and I can find spiritual significance as we bear fruit, comfort as we grow in our personal experience with the Lord.

For Meditation or Discussion

1. How have you grown through your own waiting experiences? Can you see any ways in which your character

has been strengthened or your relationship with God deepened?

2. How have you ministered to others in or through your own pain? 2 Corinthians 1:4 suggests that God "comforts us in all our troubles so that we can comfort those in any trouble with the comfort we ourselves have received from God." How have you see this in your own experience?

3. Spend some time meditating on James 5:7–8. How was the image of the farmer intended to help those in James's day who were oppressed? What additional meaning might it have for us today? How does James expand the image in 5:10–11?

12

With Thanksgiving

Today Sue often thinks, "Thank you, Lord!"

When she knew I was finally going to write this book, she told me, "Be sure you have a chapter on giving thanks."

Sue has so much to be thankful for. She says she's happier now than she has ever been in her life. Her second husband loves and accepts her—a new experience for someone who felt unloved in childhood and was deserted by her first husband. Sue today looks at her two children, now seven and four, and sees them happy and normal at last. Pat, once so destructive and hostile, is loving and sensitive, a good brother to his little sister. Pat's own inner turmoil seems gone now. Even after a three-week visit with his dad this summer, he returned home gladly, and never mentioned wanting to go live with his father.

Looking back, Sue can remember her agony while she was forced to wait on God's timing. But she can see God's hand in those months and years. She realizes that God's timing was just right, balancing every need in her life and in the lives of her children. It hurt so much to wait. But without the waiting, yesterday's pain would never have given birth to today's joy. Sue recognizes God at work in every circumstance. She acknowledges his love. And she often gives thanks.

Much of Sue's expression of thanksgiving has an Old Testament flavor.

The Hebrew words typically translated "thank" and "thanksgiving" in our English versions are *yôdah* and its derivative *tôdâh*. Actually, the Hebrew concept is different from our English "thanks," for our word tends to emphasize gratitude. The Hebrew words emphasize acknowledgment or public declaration.

Sue's experience of thanksgiving doesn't lack the emotion of gratitude. But it is distinctive because her feelings and words of thanks grow from her awareness that it really is God who has acted in her life. It really is God, shaping and timing the events, who is the source of her blessing and her joy. Sue's thanks recognize and acknowledge God's hand, and therefore become an expression of praise.

Thanksgiving as praise is something we meet often in the Psalms. One of David's psalms, recorded for us in 1 Chronicles 16, shows clearly how intimately associated thanksgiving is with acknowledgment of God's activity in our world:

Give thanks to the Lord, call on his name;
    make known among the nations what he has done.
Sing to him, sing praise to him;
    tell of all his wonderful acts.
Glory in his holy name;
    let the hearts of those who seek the Lord rejoice.
Look to the Lord and his strength;
    seek his face always.
Remember the wonders he has done,
    his miracles, and the judgments he pronounced,
O descendants of Israel his servant,
    O sons of Jacob, his chosen ones (1 Chron. 16:8–13).

Psalm 107 expresses the same theme. Following an initial call to "give thanks to the Lord, for he is good; his love endures forever" (Ps. 107:1), the psalmist outlines a number of desperate needs that we human beings experience. After each description, he presents God as one who acts to meet these needs and repeats:

> Let them give thanks to the Lord for his unfailing love
> and his wonderful deeds for men (Ps. 107:8, 15, 21, 31).

Sue's concern with thanksgiving has an Old Testament quality because, in insisting that I write about it, she is urging you and me to recognize and acknowledge God's "wonderful deeds" for us. And how important this is! When God's timing is right and all the good things he intends for us have finally come, how good it is to acknowledge God's wisdom in causing us to wait! How good it is to praise him, affirming that even our pain is now recognized as a loving gift, the seed from which our present happiness has grown!

It *is* good to give thanks to the Lord and to "make known among the nations what he has done." As we "remember the wonders he has done" for us, our own lives are enriched, and the Lord receives the praise that is his due.

Pam is praising now, too. Her life has fresh direction and she feels buoyant and thankful. It is, I suppose, easy for Sue and Pam to have a thankful attitude and to show gratitude. Each feels that one of her life's most painful waits is past. Each feels that God has acted and by his action brought relief.

But Lil, still in the grip of her fear and depression, can't sense God's hand in her situation. Yet thanksgiving is something that Lil needs to learn as well.

As we move into the New Testament, we find a different thought where our English versions speak of "thank" and "thankful" and "thanksgiving." The Greek root (*eucharist*) has the meaning of a thankful attitude as well as a show of gratitude. Strikingly, the New Testament teaches us that a thankful attitude and a show of gratitude toward God is always appropriate, even when we hurt too much to wait any longer. As Paul writes to the Thessalonians, it is the Christian's privilege to "be joyful always; pray continually; give thanks in all circumstances, for this is God's will for you in Christ Jesus" (1 Thess. 5:16–18). Even Lil—and even you and I when waiting hurts the most—can experience joy as we find encouragement in prayer and "give thanks in all circumstances."

Lil doesn't feel thankful right now.

Lil feels fear and despair.

But even now, feeling as she does, Lil can show gratitude to God by expressing her thanks.

What does Lil have to be thankful for? What kind of gratitude are you and I to feel when we, too, hurt and waiting seems only agony? In the New Testament our appreciation for the Lord has three primary associations:

(1) *Giving thanks is linked with the communion service, the eucharist.* The Bible tells us that the night Jesus was betrayed he took bread and, "when he had given thanks," broke it and said, "This is my body, which is for you." Then he took a cup, calling it "the new covenant in my blood" (1 Cor. 11:24–26). Looking back on that night of anguish, which flowed all too soon into the day of crucifixion, each account in the Gospels emphasizes the fact that Jesus "gave thanks" (cf. Matt. 26; Mark 14; Luke 22).

While you and I give thanks today for all that the suffering of Jesus won for us, this is not the emphasis in the text. There the emphasis is that *Jesus* gave thanks. It was his body about to be broken. And Jesus expressed thanks. It was his blood about to be shed. And Jesus expressed thanks.

Jesus wasn't grateful for the pain. He did not feel thankful for the weight of sin he was about to bear. But Jesus was grateful to God and thankful *in* his suffering. The Bible tells us that in his suffering Jesus simply trusted himself to God, "who judges justly." He then "bore our sins in his body on the tree, so that we might die to sins and live for righteousness; by his wounds you have been healed" (1 Pet. 2:23–24). Jesus trusted the Father to bring good from the pain, and the good that God worked through Jesus' death was our salvation.

In the same context, the Bible tells us that we, too, will have times of suffering. When these come, we are to look to Jesus, who left us "an example, that you should follow in his steps" (1 Pet. 2:21).

Jesus hurt.

But he kept on doing good.

And Jesus offered thanks to God, acknowledging with gratitude the certainty that the Father's will is just and good.

This is how you and I can react when it hurts us too much to wait. We can hurt. But we can keep on doing good. And we can acknowledge God as a loving Person and give thanks.

(2) *Giving thanks is also linked in the New Testament with the fellowship of faith.* Paul often reports that he gives thanks for others who have come to know Jesus and become the believing community (cf. Phil. 1:3; 1 Thess. 1:2, 2:13; etc.). Despite his own difficulties, Paul kept his vision of ultimate values clear. Life's central issue is found in relationship with Jesus. How thankful we too can be that we and others we know and love have discovered the eternal life that God offers all in Jesus Christ.

But Paul's prayers and thanksgiving for other believers flow from more than a common salvation. They flow from the fact that there is a unique fellowship to be found in our faith, a true partnership rooted in the Gospel. Our times of waiting will be times of pain. But God has not asked us to wait alone. He has given us a family of fellow believers—brothers and sisters who can be alongside. Brothers and sisters who will care, who will pray, who will support us in our times of waiting.

This resource is there for us even though we may not take advantage of it. When we do reach out and sense the support of a loving Christian community, we too are moved with Paul to "thank my God every time I remember you" (Phil. 1:3).

(3) *In the New Testament, thanks are associated with the blessings which have come to us through Christ.* "Thanks be to God," Paul exclaims in 1 Cor. 15:57, "he gives us the victory through our Lord Jesus Christ." In his second letter to the Corinthians, Paul adds these two thoughts: "thanks be to God, who always leads us in triumphal procession in Christ" and "thanks be to God for his indescribable gift" (2 Cor. 2:14, 9:15). In our relationship with Jesus, you and I are victors, whatever our circumstances.

The basic conviction that we are destined for good is expressed in Romans 8. After the famous "in all things God works for the good of those who love him" (v. 28), the Apostle adds, "He who did not spare his own Son, but gave him up for us all—how will he not also, along with him, graciously give us all things" (v. 32). The demonstration of God's love for us in Jesus is so totally compelling that Paul is convinced "all things" good are ours. The God who did not withhold his own Son will not withhold any good thing from us.

So we can feel gratitude—and give thanks—because we know that God's love for us is abundant and firm. Even our trials must then be an expression of love, a gift whose goodness will be understood when time has passed and we have the perspective which enables us to see the whole.

Is gratitude possible for someone like Lil? Is it realistic

to express thanks, and have a thankful attitude, even when our waiting hurts so much now? The Bible's answer is a joyful "Yes!" It is not only possible, but right.

- We can be thankful, as Jesus was, for we know that God is a just and loving Person. The first source of our gratitude is our appreciation for God himself.
- We can be thankful, as Paul was, for fellow believers. God has not left us to hurt alone. There is a fellowship of faith, a community of love, a sharing partnership for our hurts and joys.
- We can be thankful, ultimately, because in Jesus God has fully demonstrated the extent of his love. Looking at Jesus, remembering his sufferings, and knowing that his sacrifice was for us assures us that we are truly loved despite our present circumstances.

When you and I focus our thoughts on the Lord and on all that he has done for us, gratitude can fill our hearts, and we can know a joy that exists independently of our circumstances.

So today, Sue can say, "Thank you, Lord."

Today Pam can echo, "Thank you, Lord."

And even Lil, despite the fact that her wait isn't over yet, can join the chorus: "Thank you, Lord."

This book began with a quote from Ecclesiastes, a quote which suggests that there is a time for everything. It ends with another quote, from a psalm, which reminds you and me that it is always time for us to give thanks. It is time to give thanks when we are waiting. It is time to give thanks when God's timing decrees that our wait is over. So let us join the psalmist and give thanks:

Give thanks to the Lord, for he is good.

His love endures forever.

Give thanks to the God of gods.
His love endures forever.
Give thanks to the Lord of lords:
His love endures forever.
to him who alone does great wonders,
His love endures forever.
who by his understanding made the heavens,
His love endures forever.
who spread out the earth upon the waters,
His love endures forever.
who made the great lights—
His love endures forever.
the sun to govern the day,
His love endures forever.
the moon and stars to govern the night;
His love endures forever.
to him who struck down the firstborn of Egypt
His love endures forever.
and brought Israel out from among them
His love endures forever.
with a mighty hand and outstretched arm;
His love endures forever.
to him who divided the Red Sea asunder
His love endures forever.
and brought Israel through the midst of it,
His love endures forever.
but swept Pharaoh and his army into the Red Sea;
His love endures forever.
to him who led his people through the desert,
His love endures forever.
who struck down great kings,
His love endures forever. . . .
And gave their land as an inheritance,
His love endures forever.
an inheritance to his servant Israel;
His love endures forever.
to the One who remembered us in our low estate
His love endures forever.

and freed us from our enemies,
>   *His love endures forever.*
and who gives food to every creature.
>   *His love endures forever.*
Give thanks to the God of heaven.
>   *His love endures forever* (Ps. 136).

For Meditation or Discussion

1. What good things are there in your life now for which you are thankful? Looking back, can you recognize God's hand in providing your blessings? What ways can you express your thanks in the Old Testament sense of public acknowledgment and praise?

2. The New Testament sense of thanksgiving emphasizes a grateful attitude and expression of appreciation. Which of the three New Testament associations with thanks explained in this chapter is most likely to help you feel thankful even in difficult circumstances?

3. The chapters of this book have explored many different ways in which God's timing can be viewed as good, even when waiting is most painful. Which of the insights discussed has been most helpful to you?

4. Psalm 136 provides a pattern by which you can praise God and affirm his steadfast love. If you were writing such a psalm, using events from your life in place of events from Israel's history, what would you include? Why not write a psalm of thanks, using this pattern, to express your appreciation for all God has done for you.